CARING HANDS

CARING HANDS

INSPIRING STORIES OF
VOLUNTEER MEDICAL MISSIONS

Susan J. Alexis

Fairview Press
Minneapolis

Published by Fairview Press, 2450 Riverside Avenue, Minneapolis, Minnesota 55454. Fairview Press is a division of Fairview Health Services, a community-focused health system affiliated with the University of Minnesota and providing a complete range of services, from the prevention of illness and injury to care for the most complex medical conditions. For a free current catalog of Fairview Press titles, please call toll-free 1-800-544-8207. Or visit our Web site at www.fairviewpress.org.

Library of Congress Cataloging-in-Publication Data
Alexis, Susan J.
    Caring hands : inspiring stories of volunteer medical missions / Susan
J. Alexis.
        p. ; cm.
    ISBN 1-57749-128-9 (trade pbk. : alk. paper)
    1. Missions, Medical--Anecdotes. 2. Medical assistance,
American--Anecdotes. 3. War--Relief of sick and wounded--Anecdotes. 4.
Public health--International cooperation--Anecdotes. 5.
Volunteers--Anecdotes. I. Title. [DNLM: 1. Missions and
Missionaries--Personal Narratives. 2. Missions and
Missionaries--Popular Works. 3. Voluntary Workers--Personal Narratives.
4. Voluntary Workers--Popular Works. 5. Medical Missions,
Official--Personal Narratives. 6. Medical Missions, Official--Popular
Works. W 323 A384c 2003]
    RA394 .A43 2003
    610.69′5--dc21
                    2002014234

First Printing: February 2003
Printed in the United States of America
07 06 05 04 03   6 5 4 3 2 1

Funding and support for *Caring Hands: Inspiring Stories of Volunteer Medical Missions* provided by the Fairview Foundation.

Cover by Laurie Ingram Design (www.laurieingramdesign.com)
Cover photos courtesy of Karen Easterday, Monica Lindlief, Sharon Hall, and Dr. Douglas Sill
Interior by Dorie McClelland, Spring Book Design

Fairview Press publications do not necessarily reflect the philosophy of Fairview Health Services.

To my parents,
who taught me by example
the warmth of compassion,
the honor of dignity,
the strength of integrity,
the joy of service,
the beauty of giving.

"Through the hands of such as these God speaks,
and from behind their eyes He smiles upon the earth."

Kahlil Gibran, *The Prophet,* "On Giving"

Contents

Photographs

Introduction

Ecuador. From earliest memory, he has suffered the taunts of children and the stares of strangers. Deformed from birth by a cleft lip and palate, he eats with difficulty while uncontrolled drool wets his shirt. He has recently heard unbelievable news that may change his life, and he has walked a long way to see if it can be true. Now he lies face up, asleep, unaware of the buzzing flies and the motions around him.

Gloved but gownless in the intense tropical heat, a Fairview surgeon prepares to operate.

The beginnings of Fairview lie in two hospitals rooted deep in Minnesota soil and supported by solid Lutheran constituencies. The Lutheran Deaconess Hospital, so named for the Norwegian women who founded it in the late nineteenth century, reflected the sense of mission brought by these dedicated women, running not so much on the principles of good business as on those basic to strong commitment. The original Fairview Hospital, of local Lutheran founding, opened its doors nearly three decades later. In time, it proved the more dominant of the two, conferring its name on the new system when the hospitals merged in 1973. Over the years, the addition of good business people steered the merged system onto a wise financial track while retaining the sense of commitment and mission.

During those early years, everyone, recalls John Nilsen, current president of the Medical Missions Committee, felt a part of the organization and its Christian heritage. Carl Platou, the director, remained personally involved with medical staff and patients alike, walking the halls, visiting the lounge, sometimes calling people at home to ask for input as he developed his vision of expansion to the suburbs. As the system grew, employees took with them to new locations the hospital's core values: compassion, dignity, integrity, and service.

In 1987, the Fairview Foundation was created to raise funds to further Fairview's goal of bettering the health of the communities it served. Norm Groth, the Foundation's first executive director, oversaw and encouraged an expansion of the Christian service espoused by Fairview combined with new medical opportunities. His core personal values reflected those of many employees: service to other people; taking Sunday attitudes to work; staying the course after making a commitment. In like manner, the spiritual centrality embodied in John Nilsen's tireless involvement assured the Foundation's progression along these lines. The concept of the community that Fairview served moved beyond regional borders.

Kosovo. Crumbled facades and shattered windows remain from the middle class existence once enjoyed by the villagers of Semetisht. The war changed everything. Now several families share a rebuilt home while doctors and nurses still have no place from which to work. Community members and foreigners work together to build a four-room clinic.

Squatting in tennis shoes, work pants, and a casual white blouse, a Fairview therapist carefully aligns another tile on the clinic floor.

Consistent with its Lutheran heritage, Fairview has a long history of missions. Mary Baich, former Foundation director and a Californian, notes the higher rate of church attendance and interest in overseas missions found in Minnesota. Perhaps the long, dark winters encourage Northerners to do something different in a milder climate.

More simply put, people just feel the desire to give back, believes a physician who has been going on medical missions for nearly twenty years. This spirit of giving forms part of the Fairview culture, as witnessed by the many employees who donate vacation time (worth money) to raise funds for the Foundation. This spirit has proved contagious, increasing throughout the organization with every year.

Employee giving through medical missions rewards not only recipients in developing countries, but Fairview as well. Those who donate their time and efforts abroad return to share new points of view with their coworkers. Having seen how little other people have and how much we have, they rethink purposes and principles, bringing new perspectives like new blood into the organization. They return as better employees, more appreciative of the medical facilities and opportunities available here. Their excitement at living and working in another country and culture percolates through the hospitals and clinics as they tell tales and relate experiences that encourage coworkers to consider a medical mission of their own.

For volunteers, the rewards include adventure, increased cultural awareness, satisfaction at helping those less fortunate. Yet the major reason for giving remains the belief in what this can accomplish. Givers believe that their giving makes a difference.

Sudan. The sun blazes down on a landscape of dirt, rustic huts, and a few scattered trees. One in a sea of gaunt, semiclothed bodies, a mother of indecipherable age, eyes dulled by hunger, holds a scrawny baby in her lap. She dips a bony finger into a small bowl of gruel, then lifts her finger to her mouth. Again, she dips into the bowl, this time using her finger as a spoon for her baby.

As an unexpected shadow momentarily blocks the sun, she looks up into the eyes of a Fairview nurse.

Norm Groth encouraged medical missions long before the existence of a committee to regulate them. Organized events featured speakers working outside the United States in medically related fields. Occasional meetings made a point of honoring such people. These reunions remained light and enjoyable, with the goal of making listeners want to return to hear more and perhaps eventually to volunteer themselves.

As more people began to ask the Foundation for financial help to go on foreign missions, the need became obvious for greater sophistication in reviewing applicants, overseeing allocated funds, and following up after each mission. Who was going, and where? What were they doing? What were the results of their labors? To meet this need, the Foundation created the Medical Missions Committee in 1997. Its threefold purpose consists of overseeing the application process for financial assistance, publicizing the mission and funding opportunities available, and coordinating and gathering drugs and donations for those going on a medical mission.

At one time, the Medical Missions Committee received a request to focus all its energy in a single direction, allocating total funding to missions in one particular country. The answer came back a definitive no. The Medical Missions Committee, notes Mary Baich, moves on an energy all its own. Formed of people who are passionate about missions and guided by John Nilsen's vision and steadfast commitment, it needs no encouragement to expand the sharing of local skills, techniques, and supplies with diverse parts of the world.

Those eligible to apply for a Foundation grant, which may cover travel or supply requests for a medical mission, include Fairview's seventeen thousand employees, its volunteers, and physician associates sending patients to Fairview hospitals. They must travel with and work under the sponsoring direction of a recognized organization. They must also express a definite purpose in going and turn in a report of their experiences and reactions upon their return.

Sponsoring organizations, which may be religious or secular, range from those that treat a particular ailment (Operation Smile) to those that treat the masses (Volunteers in Medical Missions). Work ranges from dispensing vitamins to performing major operations, from comforting children in an orphanage to teaching foreign doctors new techniques, from building medical clinics to repairing antiquated equipment.

Although many people remain unaware of the medical missions that Fairview encourages and sponsors, the organization would be different without them, reflects Mary Baich. While only some one hundred people participate—many repeatedly—in foreign missions, their impact abroad and at Fairview grows ever greater.

Israel. Augusta Victoria Hospital in Jerusalem sits atop the Mount of Olives. As if infected by the strife around it, the hospital suffers financial and staffing difficulties. It needs experienced advisors, people willing to work in the hospital and see the problems firsthand. Administrators put in two calls to the United States. A hospital system in Chicago answers the first.

Fairview answers the second.

Heroic? That's one word for them, but *selfless* might serve better, believes Norm Groth. Missiongoers pay a price, living in rustic conditions, giving up vacation time, raising money, and sharing their talents with strangers who cannot repay them. They're the kind of people, he says, you like to have around when you need help.

Their future looks good. Fairview remains committed to adding topnotch people not only from the financial side, but from the religious, caring side, people who share the values that have guided the organization from its simple beginnings, through its expansion to a major medical system, to its affiliation with the University of Minnesota. These values bloom through expanding medical missions. Says Mary Baich, "I hope to go myself someday."

These are the tales of some who already have.

Bolivia

Andean Rural Health Care (Curamericas)

Documenting a Difference

"This work is more rewarding than you could possibly imagine."

SHARON HALL

REGISTERED NURSE

I came to know Andean Rural Health Care through a former member of my church. A group of us had been looking for an international health project, and this seemed to fit the bill. Bolivia, the country in which it operated, was home to some of the poorest people in South America. The organization—Methodist in some respects—received support from churches, businesses, and both the American and Bolivian governments.

It provided a means for native Bolivians and American volunteers to work side by side for two weeks on projects that would provide lasting benefit to local communities. In this sparsely populated world of high altitude and thin air, we built health posts in communities that had none. Someone local would donate the land. Another would offer to carry rocks from the river for the foundation. Others would promise so many hours of work. Having no machinery, the men and women performed all the labor by hand—carrying, digging, making bricks.

Back home we would raise money for the lumber, windows, tin roof, and rafters, and for the hire of a Bolivian carpenter to supervise the work. If the foundation was prepared by the time we arrived, we could put up the walls of adobe blocks already made by the local people, who would later stucco and paint them white and then finish with a corrugated tin roof.

Each health post consisted of four rooms: an exam room, a waiting room, a room with a cot for the staff to stay in, and a small kitchen. Each room had one window. There was also a bathroom, although in many cases it lacked plumbing. Fairview provided a grant to cover many of the medicines and medical supplies we donated. The Bolivian government provided free vaccines.

Everyone on the team spent time building or repairing, and we alternated taking mornings off to go with Bolivian health workers from rural home to rural home taking a health census. We walked through sparse fields of potatoes and beans, there being no roads from one lonely house to another. At thirteen thousand feet, the mountainous terrain displayed fields on incredibly steep slopes, scattered patches here and there, laboriously plowed with oxen or by hand. The thin soil and arid climate permitted only stunted crops, which would have yielded richer harvests under better conditions.

The subsistence farmers and their families lived in single-story, adobe block homes, frequently painted turquoise, with windows too few and small to allow much light inside. More prosperous farmers owned small two-story houses with the family living on the second floor, the livestock taking over the ground floor in cold weather.

The censuses of Andean Rural Health Care record important data regarding Bolivian health and living conditions. Census takers weigh children, give shots, teach mothers to boil drinking water and how to keep alive a baby suffering from diarrhea. For each individual, they note age, health status, shots given, their water source, and whether plumbing exists. They also ask questions regarding the possibilities of general health education. Is there perhaps a radio in the house or another means of communication with the outside world?

Andean Rural Health Care operates through the local community. Bolivians form the board of directors. Working with them time and again has been like visiting old friends. We donate our medical supplies to the headquarters in La Paz, which distributes them among the poorly equipped health posts. In 1990, most didn't have an X-ray machine, although they did have the capability to draw blood. Inadequate though they are, they provide the only medical service available to people who would otherwise have none. A person with perhaps two years of training, somewhat comparable to a licensed practical nurse, runs each post. That person trains literate individuals from the local community in basic first aid, how to give shots, and the general hygienic education he or she must communicate to the families visited during the census.

An especially poignant incident stands out from my many trips to Bolivia. The people of a rural community had taken in a fifteen-year-old orphan girl. Sick and too weak to walk, she showed symptoms pointing to tuberculosis. We drove her to the nearest hospital, an Italian-funded institution forty-five minutes away. It actually had X-ray equipment, beds, nurses, and doctors. The hospital diagnosed TB in the girl's lungs and abdomen. Even though I am a nurse, I had never seen an active case of this disease.

In a culture that is so family oriented, where relatives frequently move into the hospital along with the patient, this girl had no one to accompany her. The unpleasant medicine for tuberculosis makes people sick. Unless they remain under medical supervision, uneducated people tend to stop taking it, facilitating the bacteria's resistance to future antibiotic treatment. Doctors worried that with no one to stay with her, the girl might leave as soon as she was able. I can still see her, extremely thin, her hair uncombed and unwashed for weeks, in the typical layers of skirts and petticoats, no socks, rubbery sandals made from old tires, a sweater, and a shawl. I did not see her again, but I heard talk later about her being an angel, so I knew that she had died.

I have traveled to Bolivia five times since 1990, each time revisiting the same area although not necessarily the same community. On my first census, one out of three children under the age of five had died. By the last census, the statistics had improved dramatically, showing a reduction in infant mortality by over one-third and in deaths of children under five by over one-half. I realized that I was documenting not only better health but living proof that we were making a difference. Our vaccinations, our education on boiling water and saving babies with diarrhea was slowly changing the lives of these people. When I first went, many women had eight or ten pregnancies, but only three children over the age of five to show for it. They bore numerous children because they knew a high percentage would die. Now they need to think about family planning, because babies don't die as often as they used to. Unfortunately, in this uneducated milieu, people remain suspicious of any means to prevent pregnancy, thinking it might be a government plot. The Catholic Church stands against contraception as well.

Americans commonly suffer from altitude sickness on landing in La Paz. Getting to bed fast has proved the best cure for the headache and nausea, which normally last only twenty-four hours. Taking altitude medicine in advance and for three or four days while there also helps. It doesn't work for everyone, however. We learn to live with the shortness of breath in this low-oxygen environment. If we are shoveling or carrying big stones, we have to pace ourselves and move slowly.

Time-conscious Americans have to fight the frustration of not being able to work quickly. We stop and rest every hour. Physically, I now find myself past the hard work of laboring in a high altitude environment, yet this work is more rewarding than you could possibly imagine. In the future, I will go to other needy areas, perhaps in the southwest border area of our own country.

Andean Rural Health Care proved so successful that it was taken over completely by Bolivians, who continue to run it on their own. This provides a wonderful example of helping people to help themselves. The American side of Andean Rural Health Care is now called Curamericas, and has expanded its operations throughout Latin America and the southwestern border of the United States.

When local people and American volunteers finish building a medical outpost, they celebrate with a potluck. The community presents the volunteers with a plaque listing the names of those who have contributed to the building. This plaque is nailed to the wall of the outpost, thus perpetuating the thanks of Bolivians to those who came from another country to help them. In this manner, I am a part of at least three health posts on the altiplano.

More than that, I am a part of unknown children who didn't die, thanks to hygienic education, to which I contributed. I am a part of anyone brought back to health in an outpost I helped to build. And, of many rural Bolivians who remember Americans with kind thoughts, I am also a part.

Kosovo

World Servants

Sharing over a Cup of Coffee

*"What would I do if in my hometown all the houses were burned,
all the businesses were gone, all the gardens were destroyed?"*

KRISTEN MCWILLIAMS

CARDIAC REHABILITATION THERAPIST

World Servants, an international nondenominational Christian organization, identifies areas of humanitarian need and develops relationships with people by partnering with a given community. Rather than forming its own agenda, it asks the community: What do you need to improve your life? Where, when, and how do you want help? It provides teams to work alongside the residents—with them, not for them. Local people direct the project.

Training for a World Servants project includes two orientation classes that teach prospective team members about the culture they will enter and enjoin them to respect local beliefs and traditions. While volunteers perform humanitarian work in the Christian spirit, they make no attempt to impose their own set of cultural or faith-based beliefs or to change those of others. For example, ethnic Albanian Kosovars, being mostly Muslim, use the Old Testament but not the New. Village elders forbade us to use it in games or any other activities. We respected their wishes, thereby increasing our credibility and earning their trust. When we offered to help furnish the medical clinic we had built during my second trip, we anticipated an antiseptic and functional setup, yet we remained respectful when the Kosovars chose attractiveness instead. We waited until asked to share our views.

Because of the way the organization works to develop relationships between Americans and local people, the Kosovars asked us about our beliefs more than we had expected. Working together leads to trust and confidence, which leads to questions. This philosophy of cooperation fits well with mine. It's like sharing over a cup of coffee.

In order to build these relationships, World Servants made a five-year commitment to this community. With members of my family, I have traveled two consecutive years to the Kosovar town of Semetisht, which was hard-hit during the war with the Serbs. Its population now stands at three to four hundred. Of its 152 homes, 150 were either damaged or destroyed during the war.

Neither my husband, my teenage boys, nor I had ever traveled out of the country, except to Canada, at the time of our first trip to Kosovo. I think we all had expected a Third World country, even though our training had told us otherwise. Instead, we stepped into a middle- or working-class life made poor by the wars of the 1990s in former Yugoslavia. The mix of professionals, teachers, plumbers, shop-keepers, and farmers—sophisticated people with a once flourishing wine industry—had lived in homes similar to ours, listened to stereos, watched television, and owned small refrigerators. Now, after the war, we could find up to twenty people living in the single remaining room of a bombed-out house. The massive destruction appalled us. What would I do, I asked myself, if in my hometown all the houses were burned, all the businesses were gone, all the gardens were destroyed?

The area's long history of being overrun and conquered by various powers has taken a toll on religion as well. Many of the younger citizens, holding to the stubborn attitude that no one is going to force them to believe anything anymore, consider themselves atheists. Those who claim to be Muslim form a secular crowd, showing up in a mosque once a year, just as many Christians turn up in church on Christmas and Easter. Among the middle-aged, we encountered more adherence to Islam, while the elderly remained the most faithful.

It takes a big adjustment to fit into another culture without judging it. My boys made friends of their own age while carefully trying to follow the rigid code that rules relationships between men and women in this Muslim area. Until age twenty-two, when young women graduate from the university, they may not spend unchaperoned time with unrelated males, even to walk down the street. Everything has to be done in groups. This proved hard for my sons to remember when they asked permission to walk a girl home after school. We reminded them that such an innocent action was impermissible in Semetisht. Larger towns were moving gradually toward more Western standards, but our village remained conservative.

I encountered little of the age segregation so common in the United States. At any time, a forty-five-year-old woman might be walking with someone else's six-year-old and someone else's fourteen-year-old, all three holding hands, engaged in animated conversation, and having a good time. Kids of all ages, of course, proved themselves open to friendship, and I frequently had two hanging on my legs and one on each arm as I vainly tried to get something done.

We found the people very pro-American, largely because they believe that the United States had saved their lives by its intervention in the war. We had people literally grabbing us off the street and kissing us or pulling us into stores to serve us coffee. After the September

11 terrorist attack on the World Trade Center, we received e-mails from friends in Kosovo informing us of candlelight vigils being held there for our dead.

How did we form such lasting relationships? It began six to nine months before our trip, when advance planners from World Servants met with village elders to determine the most needy in the village and to interview those people. Recipients had to agree with World Servants' philosophy of doing *with* rather than *for*.

We team members paid a rent of $40 a day per person. World Servants sent this money in advance of our trip to help rebuild or repair damaged homes so team members could stay there. The recipients of these donations then became responsible—by contract—for housing us when we came. In some cases, they shared their homes with us. In others, they moved in with relatives for the duration of our stay, leaving their entire home to team members. Team members also raised their own airfare and money for building supplies and food, so that all the money went into the community.

On my initial trip, I spent the first week digging wells. (There still remains a need for basic clean water and sanitation, most of which was destroyed during the Serbian occupation.) I tiled bathrooms during the second week. In contrast to our American expectations, local contractors, rather than the householder, chose the tiles and bought them in Eastern Europe.

One of the bathrooms I tiled stood in the home of Sahid and Safira Hoxha. Sahid was five-foot-six and thin, with a dark complexion, brown hair and eyes, poor teeth, and a mustache. Like many village men, he wore casual Western European clothes. His wife, Safira, wore the typical half-pants, half-skirt dress of the area and often the *hajib*, the scarf so common in Eastern Europe. She followed the role reserved for women in this Muslim community: cooking, washing clothes, serving tea and coffee, then moving off into the background to be seen but not heard. She remained reserved, whether from hard work or grief, I never knew. The couple had had three children, two boys and a younger girl who suffered from a heart ailment requiring medication. When the war drove the family into a refugee camp, no medicine was available, and the little girl died at the age of eight.

Along with a young man from Pennsylvania, I was assigned to tile the Hoxha's bathroom. I heard considerable discussion among the contractors about a woman tiling a bathroom. Did I know what I was doing? Sahid appeared to share these doubts, checking on me constantly. When we finished, the astounded contractor repeated over and over, *"Shume mir!"* (Very good!) "I didn't think you could do this!" The next year on my second trip, this same contractor immediately pointed to me and decreed with as much English as he could muster, "You—tile bathrooms!"

Fairview sponsored that second trip, during which we worked to build a four-room medical clinic, one of only two clinics available for the region's eighty thousand people. The area had doctors and nurses but few places for them to work after the war. This made us grateful for the extensive medical system we enjoy in the United States.

Three consecutive teams cooperated to build the clinic. The first dug out the space, the second put up the framework and roof, and our team completed the finishing work. So much time went into construction that we had little left to actually *work* in the building. Nevertheless, the people planned a festive ribbon-cutting ceremony for the clinic opening, and two flags were raised—Kosovar and American.

My medical work in Semetisht underscored the great need for healthcare. Without exception, the diastolic pressure of every male I tested read over 100, with no blood pressure medicine available. The pharmacies had been burned out and looted. You couldn't even find a

Band-Aid. The Kosovars recognized that they suffered health problems, making their lack of available supplies and medicines all the more frustrating.

Many men asked me what they could do about their high blood pressure. Most smoked American-made, filterless cigarettes sold cheaply on the street. With no filter, the amount of nicotine the cigarettes passed into their bodies only added to their psychological addiction, smoking being one of the few postwar pleasures available. A few admitted having tried in vain to quit. Keep trying, was all I could say.

Some of the local practices amazed us. Women spoon-fed babies who were strapped down flat to their crib. I sat on the edge of my chair on more than one occasion, fearful that the baby would choke. It never happened. To lull their babies to sleep, mothers rocked their cradles with the violence of a rattle. Somehow, the babies ended up asleep and unharmed.

Medically, our concepts of modesty, propriety, patient rights, and confidentiality have no place in Kosovo, from what I saw. A local nurse and an administrator, showing me around, didn't even knock before barging into a room with a woman on a table in midlabor. I mumbled apologies; the nurse and administrator did not. Instead, they took me into another room to introduce me to a doctor in the middle of examining a male patient. The doctor left his patient forgotten and shirtless while he offered to make me a cup of Turkish coffee on the equivalent of a Bunsen burner. (This strong, sweet, highly caffeinated drink forms part and parcel of Kosovar life.) I politely declined, feeling awkward about the waiting patient.

Building and tiling the clinic gave us more visibility than our work in private houses. This led to some arguing among the village men. Some felt that the American women were out of place, setting a bad example for the local women by working outside of our homes. Others, more liberal, asked questions. "How did you learn to do this? Do you work with men in America?" I even heard the comment, "We should have more women doing this." We spoke with the village elders to be sure that they were amenable to women working like this, as we did not want to offend. We continued, with their permission, noting that they were as much impacted by our culture as we were by theirs.

One day, Sahid saw me tiling a clinic bathroom and invited my family for coffee. We talked about how my husband and I worked on everything as a team. "You know," he said finally, "I've often made fun of my wife because the only things she knows how to do are cook and wash clothes. I'm beginning to think that this has more to do with me than with her."

The typical questions asked of a woman are: Are you married? How many children do you have? How many of them are boys?

I have three boys. One woman with whom I spoke had five girls and two boys. "Oh," she sighed, "you are such a fortunate woman—so much more blessed than I am."

"Why?" I questioned. "You have seven children!"

"Yes," she replied sadly, "but only two that are worthwhile."

In extreme examples of the old culture, women remain largely silent. They enter the living room—referred to as the "men's room"—to serve, then leave. They do not work outside the home. Some high school girls and university women, however, have been influenced by what they see of other countries on television. They don't want to get married in their own region; rather, they want the greater possibilities available to them in other countries, or at least in the more Westernized cities. This new line of thought comes through in their clothing. Women over thirty, if not wearing the half-pants, half-skirt outfit, still dress modestly with a skirt below the knees and short-sleeved rather than sleeveless dresses.

The younger women, however, prefer European fashions that rival anything here in the States, sporting tight clothing and spaghetti straps.

It became hard not to speak out about the treatment of women. What seemed like discrimination to us might truly be seen by these women as "protection." Even so, in private discussions we often sensed the beginnings of change in their thinking.

There remains a darker side to this culture's view of women. In this war, as in others, women and girls were raped by opposition soldiers. It is automatically assumed that these women are guilty (sexual sin is the woman's fault) and that they are now ruined and worthless. Even in larger towns, more liberal than the villages, these sentiments prevail. Some of the sobbing confessions that we as medical people heard from victims were the only ones they will ever give. Were their families to know, they would put them out. These women live with stress, guilt, and the impossibility of ever telling even another woman in their own family about the terrible violence that was done to them.

Working in Kosovo has changed my perspective. I see the world as a more complex place. Never leaving home made it too easy to remain insular. Now I have shared the lives of people who live halfway around the world. I have tasted new foods, seen the impact of war, and smelled filthy pollution. You can't pick this up from a book.

One of my sons noted that people who ask about his trip to Kosovo remain politely interested for two or three minutes but shift the conversation after five. They have little grasp of the complexity or depth of deprivation in a war-ravaged part of the world. My son, on the other hand, considers this trip the most meaningful thing he has done in his entire life.

My concept of "problem" has changed. Clothing? Leftovers? Short staffing? None of this qualifies. Kosovo has exposed me to *real* problems—cruelty, deprivation, hatred, death. My problems are petty. When I hear people whine, I often think, "You ought to try living in Kosovo."

World Servants has now sent several teams to Semetisht, and we have made a good name for ourselves. A man from another village commented, "Oh, you're the ones from Semetisht. You're different from other Americans." I assume he was referring to the fact that we don't just drop off bricks in front of a home and drive away. We stay and work hand in hand with the people.

At one time the village elders had a choice. They could take a $150,000 grant from an Islamic organization or accept our offer of a five-year commitment to send work teams to rebuild. They chose us. That says something about the relationships we've formed.

Ecuador

Interplast

Correcting the Negative

"I want to put lipstick on two lips, not three."

JOSEPH GRYSKIEWICZ
PLASTIC SURGEON

Most people feel a need to give back. That drive arises from within oneself but may be conditioned by religion or encouraged by the milieu in which one works. I trace my repeated trips to Ecuador with Interplast to all three factors.

Seven and a half years into seminary, studying to become a priest psychologist, I heard a talk by a priest who ran a mission in Guatemala. At the conclusion, he invited anyone with an interest to go and see what he was talking about. I took him up on the offer, spending three weeks at the mission, shocked by what I saw. Sixty percent of the children of San Lucas Tolimán died before the age of five. I saw them daily at the clinic, dying of malnutrition, dying of tuberculosis. I had never witnessed anything like it, and I knew I wanted to return to help.

The conditions I had seen brought home to me the uselessness of a psychology major. What was I going to say? "I see you're depressed.

I'm sorry you've lost your three children to disease and malnutrition." Instead, I finished a nursing degree and went back for six months.

I examined a lot of children with birth defects and a lot of adults with hand injuries from badly aimed machete swings. I saw too many children with burns. The poor in Guatemala live in one-room, smoke-filled houses with an open fire in the center for cooking. Children prove frequent victims. I remember the sad case of one boy who suffered seizures and had fallen into the fire on more than one occasion. All of this compelled me to do more.

San Lucas Tolimán had no phones. One morning a man on a bicycle handed me a telegram from my fiancée. "YOU'RE IN MINNESOTA! CONGRATULATIONS!" it screamed, meaning that I had been accepted into medical school. I was beside myself, but the people there—illiterate for the most part—couldn't understand all the hullabaloo. I followed my normal custom of driving to a little village clinic that night, but on this occasion I offered to buy a beer for everyone in town. Again, no one understood my elation, but all were glad for a free beer. Uncelebrated by the world I wanted to help, I returned to the United States to become a plastic surgeon.

During my senior year of residency, the chief of surgery took us on an Interplast mission to Ecuador. Interplast, founded by plastic surgeons to help children in developing countries who have birth defects or burns, has a history of some three decades. I have been going yearly since 1984, but only in the early 1990s did I realize that Fairview not only encourages such missions but also offers financial help for travel and supply costs. Many people could not go without this assistance; in my case, this generosity has enabled me to do more.

In Ecuador, the local coordinator for Interplast puts out announcements on the radio, in the paper, and by word of mouth. In the past sixteen years we have traveled to four towns ranging in size from twenty thousand to two and a half million (Guayaquil). In all four locations, we have operated on people who have come from many miles around. One mother, having traveled thirty hours by bus, walked into the hospital holding a baby with a cleft lip. "Will you operate on my child?" she asked, searching my face. "Sure," I replied with a grin, "you betcha," as her face broke into a wide smile. Such encounters have left me hooked on this work.

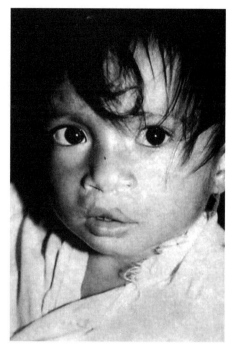

A typical team consists of two plastic surgeons, two anesthesiologists, an occupational therapist, surgery nurses, a recovery room nurse, and sometimes a speech therapist. The incidence of cleft lip and palate is much higher in Central and South America than in the United States, due, I am guessing, to malnutrition, inbreeding, and a geographical concentration of genes tending toward this defect. Ecuador offers few plastic surgeons, and the majority of people have no money to pay for them anyway. The national healthcare system remains too poor to cover all the people's needs.

There will always be cases we can't handle. Some hand injuries demand microscopic surgery. We don't dare remove really large tumors due to a lack of equipment needed to prevent bleeding to death. Some children come in so malnourished that they lack the protein necessary for healing. But mostly, we turn people down because of volume. We always tell them, "We'll come back next year," and we mean it.

Nevertheless, parents are desperate. When I come out of a surgery to tell a parent how it went, another will pull at my sleeve and plead for his or her child. When I return from lunch, two or three parents will detain me on my way in. Some, in desperation, have resorted to putting their child on any available cart and wheeling the child into the operating room themselves. To avoid operating on unexamined children, I have resorted to writing the patient's name with indelible ink on his or her arm. No name, no records—no operation.

Most patients and parents demonstrate acceptance and resignation in cases in which we absolutely can't operate. They hold a different view of life, considering themselves predestined to be poor or maimed. Many tourists I know embrace a superficial view of these poverty-stricken people. "They're happy," they say. In my view, many are clinically depressed and simply resigned to their lot rather than happy.

While I consider Ecuador better off than Guatemala, I nevertheless find myself repeatedly shocked by some of the cases I treat. A twenty-six-year-old man, his face deformed by a prominent cleft lip and palate, limped in on club feet. He couldn't talk well, walk well, or eat well. There was nothing I could do for his feet, but I fixed his lip and palate, and at least left him able to go out in society without being ridiculed for his face.

A sixteen-year-old girl with big, brown eyes and thick, black hair—a little on the pudgy side with a pink shirt and typical long skirt—begged us for a solution to her split upper lip. "I want to put lipstick on two lips, not three," she pleaded. She cried for joy the next day when she saw her reconstructed face in the mirror.

The hospitals remain primitive, with flies buzzing around the operating room, undaunted by the flyswatter we keep on the anesthesia machine. We also keep handy a large bucket of water to scrub our hands before surgery, as water may or may not be running when we need it.

Electricity is equally erratic, and in some instances we have operated with the help of nurses holding flashlights. At other times I have worked in my bare feet, as the temperature can rise above a hundred, making it too hot for either shoes or operating gown. We do the best we can under these conditions. Fortunately for our patients, the facial area has a good blood supply, keeping infection rates from cleft lip and palate surgeries very low. I worry more with burns.

Each year, the local food makes some team participants sick, basically those who don't follow the rules. Drink only water you know is boiled or bottled. Don't eat fruits or vegetables that you can't peel or cook. Don't buy food from street vendors.

While we have occasionally made use of a hotel, we generally stay for free in wealthy families' homes as arranged by the local surgeon. The first home I stayed in boasted seven servants, four guard dogs, and a guard with an Uzi who patrolled the iron-gated grounds at night. Such wealth stands in sharp contrast to the poverty of the vast majority.

This generalized poverty leads to a high crime rate. Most Ecuadorians think that all Americans are millionaires who live on streets bricked with gold. Each year, someone on the team gets robbed, usually by an unseen pickpocket. A few incidents have taken a more violent turn—a hand reaching through an open cab window to rip a gold necklace from around a woman's neck, or a pair of thieves knocking down one person while grabbing the wallet of another who tries to help. You have to be careful.

Each year I come back sick and psychotically sleep deprived, but thoroughly rewarded by my experience. I find it inexpressibly deep and meaningful to change a child's life. "Plastic" comes from the Greek word *plastikos,* meaning to shape, mold, or form. In the States, I do cosmetic surgery. I get paid well, often by picky parents who want their child to look perfect. In Ecuador, I get paid nothing by parents who are happy and thankful if I'll only take a look at their child, ecstatic if I can operate. For anything, they are profoundly grateful. I run no risk of a malpractice suit and work under less pressure. Truthfully, I have a lot of fun, and I know that in these parents' eyes, I am a hero.

The contributions I have made will remain. I have corrected a lot of negative images. By giving former outcasts a new face, I have given them the chance for a normal social life, the chance to go to school. I have unburdened their suffering parents of the commonly held belief that they must have done something wrong to have produced a deformed child.

Further, I have dispelled some of the negative images that people in developing countries have of Americans. Organizations like Interplast promote Americans as caring and generous individuals among people who too often hate us without knowing us. My public relations efforts will flower for my grandchildren.

SOUTH AFRICA

Open Arms of Minnesota, Archdiocesan AIDS Ministry

C Is for Community

"We are facing a crisis here in South Africa. Our children are dying. We need your prayers to overcome this disease."

KEVIN SHORES

PERFORMANCE IMPROVEMENT ANALYST

As a registered dietitian, I have done volunteer work related to HIV/AIDS nutrition for over ten years. When the Thirteenth International AIDS Conference was held in South Africa in 2000, representatives from various Twin Cities AIDS service organizations attended. This conference changed many of their lives, and they, in turn, changed mine, leading to my volunteer mission in South Africa. There I directed my efforts toward working with agencies that feed people living with this widespread disease.

Within a few hours of landing in South Africa, I began work with the François-Xavier Bagnoud Association, which runs programs that include home visits, childcare, and income-generating activities. Through this organization, I made home visits in Soweto and other townships outside of Johannesburg. Working in these townships proved an eye opener.

While some South African townships have areas that look like southern California, most areas do not fall into this category. "Formal" dwellings distinguish themselves by their size, durability, and internal luxuries of plumbing and electricity. "Informal" dwellings, on the other hand, consist of corrugated metal walls with no windows. Mainly they belong to squatters (of which there are many) who put their dwellings together out of any materials they can find. The typical informal family dwelling would fit into half of my single-car garage. One woman I visited had no lights in her home, which was the size of a walk-in closet. She shared the single room and one bed with her four children.

Because so many South African parents have died of AIDS, many of these tiny dwellings contain grandparents and grandchildren, or extended families of aunts and uncles, nephews and nieces. I did not see any orphanages; children often become the responsibility of their relatives or the community, adding to the strain on already thin resources.

People living in these conditions can't get out of the cold. Many have no toilet, no running water. They face difficulties with such necessities as getting transportation to the clinic or finding resources for food and school fees. Despite such trying conditions, most of these people retain their sense of humor, their generosity, and their welcoming attitude.

I visited a family whose daughter had just died. They could not hold the funeral until their other daughter arrived from Port Elizabeth, over a hundred miles away. She could not come until the next payday, when she would have enough money for the train. Meanwhile, local custom dictated that a prayer session be held every evening in the parents' home, the parents being expected to provide food for the attendees. To pay for the meals and the funeral, the bereaved parents were forced to sell their few possessions.

Through these home visits, I began to realize how the needs, resources, and cultures differed between South Africa and the United States. I stood out as a forty-two-year-old male interested in nutrition, as feeding there remains women's work.

School food programs in Guguletu, a township of some 350,000 outside of Cape Town, provided another eye opener. The primary school I visited could provide food for first through third graders, but not for fourth through seventh graders, who had to watch the younger children eat while they themselves went hungry.

A local secondary school, unable to provide any meals, asked the assistance of a pastor who runs the nearby community center. Teachers had discovered that some poverty-stricken families, unable to feed all the children in their care, had to stop feeding the ones with HIV out of necessity. Now, some twenty-four students make the five-minute walk

each day to the community center, where volunteers from the church auxiliary prepare lunch, the only daily meal many of these students will receive. On weekends, they eat nothing. Preparing sandwiches with the church volunteers allowed me to start learning phrases in Xhosa, the language used in this part of South Africa. This opened my eyes to aspects of South African culture I might otherwise have overlooked.

The fact that a white foreigner would care to learn about their culture, history, or language seemed to take many South Africans by surprise. In a Cape Town bookstore, when I requested a Xhosa-English dictionary, the employee replied, "Oh, you don't need one of those. They all speak English."

In Cape Town, our team stayed in a hotel, each of us going our different ways during the day and returning to share our experiences at night. On one of these occasions—my birthday—we were joined by an Afrikaner graduate student who was studying theology. She had joined the meal program to fulfill her year of social service. As she shared her reminiscences of growing up under apartheid, she labeled us "incredibly naive" about South African history. We ended up talking into the night about the prior centuries; the Portuguese, Dutch, English, and Huguenots; the apartheid system that sent men to work the mines and the farms, to live in barracks away from their families (who weren't allowed); the consequent spreading of sexually transmitted diseases; the strain on the family unit; the lack of job opportunities at home; the disempowerment of women.

The young woman's remarks were echoed by a Michigan nun working in Johannesburg. The apartheid system, she explained, had mandated a hierarchical division into white, colored, and black, not only in living areas and employment, but in education as well. This nun's efforts, along with those of others, were directed toward replacing the triplicate educational system with a single one for all. "America is not very challenging," she told me. "Just look at what we're working with over here."

The carryover from years of apartheid hinders progress for all South Africans. In many city councils now mixed black Africans refuse to speak Afrikaans, the language of white oppression; Afrikaners refuse to speak Xhosa, the language of the local black community. Yet all are multilingual, as even little ones in daycare begin to learn a third and fourth language at that tender age.

Nor is it culturally acceptable to talk about sex. A schoolteacher confided to me that she could talk more easily about AIDS prevention with her students than with her own daughters. Fear of AIDS is all-pervasive. If a woman chooses not to breastfeed her baby, the people around her are likely to wonder "Why not? Does she have AIDS?"

I had the opportunity to visit the Philani Nutrition Center, which began its fight against hunger and malnutrition twenty years ago in another township outside of Cape Town. It has since expanded to include job training, daycare, a meal program for women and their children, and a visiting nurse program. Here women learn to weave, a vital means of support for themselves and their families, as unemployment in many townships runs above 60 percent. The center receives charitable donations from several world churches, but no government funding.

I also toured Brown's Farm Clinic outside of Cape Town, the only clinic available for the 300,000 people living there. While public health nutrition as we know it does not exist in South Africa, the clinic does offer a small food program, as well as the services of physicians for two hours a day. Nurses and nurse practitioners run the clinic from 8:00 A.M. to 5:00 P.M. Patients begin lining up at 4:00 in the morning knowing they will be triaged. They realize that, despite having stood in line for hours, they may not be seen.

I met Beauty on one of our Guguletu home visits. Her husband was dead. Her parents were dead. Her sister, brother, and nephew had been buried on three consecutive Saturdays. She cared for five of their orphaned children as well as three of her own. In her early thirties, with no visible means of support, she remained home, unable to work. Her chronic fatigue and emaciated body testified to the ravages of the disease that was killing her. We checked in every few days and brought groceries, as the house had no food. Yet Beauty considered herself more fortunate than most.

"I am very lucky," she told me one day, her head slightly raised on the pillow.

"How so?" I asked.

"I have medicine."

I looked around, puzzled, considering the abject poverty in which she lived. "What medicine?" I wondered aloud.

She smiled as she considered her good fortune. "I have aspirin," she replied.

She died a month after I returned home.

Guguletu offers one maternity hospital and one day hospital (no overnight beds) for its 350,000 citizens. Five-year-old Sbongile lay on a bed in the hospital ward I visited on Valentine's Day. A dozen children lay in the open AIDS ward. Sbongile had come in suffering from one of its many complications. Her parents had already died of the disease; an aunt was raising her. We brought toys and hugs to brighten up her day. Two months later, the little girl was dead.

Back in Minnesota, I received a letter from Goodman Pehana, one of the many friends I made in South Africa. He wrote, "Last Saturday at JL Zwane church, we had three coffins. All were young people, victims of AIDS. We are facing a crisis here in South Africa. Our children are dying. We need your prayers to overcome this disease."

C is for "communication." Since my return from South Africa, I've talked a lot about what I did. Those who tell me I wasted my time and money on this effort are not really interested in hearing what I have to say. Did I make a huge impact in dealing with AIDS in South Africa? Probably not. Did I make a dent? Without a doubt, yes. Furthermore, I sent regular e-mails detailing our work to be posted on the Fairview Web site. I've talked to a couple hundred Minnesotans about what I saw, what I did, and what needs to be done. I've raised awareness.

We grow immensely as we learn about ourselves and our own culture by leaving it and entering another. C is also for "community"—the neighborhood, the city, the region, the country, the hemisphere, the world. We need to look at community as incorporating all of humanity.

Kevin Shores was the recipient of the 2002 Fairview Cares Award.

Mexico

Youth Adventures

A Passion for This Work

"Physically, the children showed only normal kid-type ailments.
We just gave them the love and attention kids everywhere should have."

ANGELA ENGLISH

REGISTERED NURSE

My singles group at First Baptist Church in Minneapolis was an active one. In 1998, seven of us joined with a group from another church and contacted Youth Adventures, an organization that sends teenagers on work projects. They agreed to try young adults and arranged for us to work at two orphanages in Monterrey, Mexico.

Monterrey lies in Mexico's arid north. More modernized and Americanized than most Mexican cities, it claims status as the country's third largest. Our team stayed in a seminary on a nearby mountainside, battling mosquitoes and shrieking under the cold water in the showers, but enjoying the gorgeous mountain views. Each day, some of us remained at the seminary to build bunk beds while others drove to the in-town orphanage in dilapidated, overheating vans lent to Youth Adventures by helpful Mexicans.

A tall iron gate at the sidewalk in front of the orphanage opened into a courtyard, which could have been attractive had it contained grass or flowers. As it was, a slab of gray cement surrounded an old fountain that no longer worked. On the lower floor of the building, a single large room served as both school and dining room; a small office and kitchen lay off to one side. Upstairs, the single undivided room contained cots pushed up like dominoes against the walls, enough for the twenty-two children ranging in age from six months to twelve years. At any one time, only two caregivers were present.

The backyard, like the front, consisted of a gray cement slab running up against the typical Mexican wall that divided one building from another. Clotheslines crisscrossed the yard, and a single washer stood against the building. In the course of the week, our group replaced the rickety outside stairs so that the children could come safely and directly from the upper floor into the backyard.

I deposited the stock of first-aid supplies I had brought for the orphanages, then began some assessments. Physically, the children showed only normal, kid-type ailments. We just gave them the love and attention kids everywhere should have. The first day, they cried when we left, but they greeted us with laughter and hugs when we returned the next morning.

It took a subsequent day trip to get us to the second orphanage, located in a mountain village. The boys' dorm there, absolutely atrocious, smelled like a barn. I noted that the children were smaller for their age than those we had seen in Monterrey, and many had the sniffles. The owners shared a moving account of how the orphanage had come into some extra money, which the adults had planned to use for bunk beds so the children would no longer have to sleep two to a bed. The children, on hearing the proposition, had urged that the money be sent instead to children in Chiapas, the poverty-stricken Mexican state

that has suffered several years of guerrilla warfare. How incredibly generous and utterly unselfish, I thought. In comparison, how much I have and how little I really need! Our idea of poverty in the United States doesn't even compare to what I saw with these children in Mexico.

The children in this second orphanage attended public school, so only those under age five received our visit. In the girls' dorm I found a little two- or three-year-old: pug nose, black eyes, and black hair with little flip curls at the end. She wore a pink sweater but walked barefoot, something I wouldn't have wanted any child of mine to do in that cool temperature. I spoke no Spanish, but I played and made her laugh. She grabbed my hand and began to lead me—to where, I didn't know. We exited the building around to the side and came to an old swing set, where the little girl indicated she wanted to be pushed. I complied, of course.

This mission experience opened a door that changed my life. I didn't grow up in a church that stressed missions. When I went to Mexico, I was twenty-nine and had never been on a mission trip before. Learning how to raise the needed funds taught me how generous people really are. Many donors couldn't be a part of the trip but nevertheless wanted to help. Fairview contributed funds for the first-aid supplies and travel costs. The experience made me want to quit my job, sell my house and car, and take off on another mission. I realized that I had a passion for this work.

A year and a half later, I started dating a man who takes mission groups overseas. I'm married now, and my passion for mission has become part of my life. I call in when I'm available to work, serving part-time in hospital pediatrics and home hospice, leaving my summers free for mission work. Last summer, we took a group of eighty volunteers across the Atlantic to Scotland, where the official church, claimed only by the old, has given up on trying to attract the youth. We haven't.

On my original mission to Monterrey, I didn't know how I would interact with people in a new culture. I didn't even speak Spanish, but I loved kids. Loving a child for a week—in which he or she wouldn't otherwise have known that love—forced me out of my boxed concept of who I am and what I can do. It taught me that God uses anybody who is willing.

ΠEPAL

Helping Hands, Himalayan Rescue Association

Repaying the Debt

"We slept together in a pile in a single room on a dirt floor, and everyone slept well. The phone never rang because there wasn't one."

DOUGLAS SILL

FAMILY PRACTITIONER

The little country of Nepal sits among the highest mountains on earth. It was these that first attracted me to this spot on the other side of the globe, but it was the beauty of the people that drew me back in 1995. I returned not to vacation, but to work. This time I stayed for five months and brought with me medicines, medical equipment, and my entire family.

Various factors combined to facilitate the adventure. Professionally, I had worked enough years at my clinic to earn a sabbatical. I had connected with Helping Hands, an organization bringing help to Nepal through Western physicians. My children had reached appropriate ages—Justin, fourteen; Nathan, eleven; Adam, nine; and Zak, seven. Sharon, my wife, who had known from the beginning of our marriage that I dreamed of repaying what I considered a debt for the medical skills I had been privileged to learn, became a willing partner.

Our primary concern centered around the education of our boys. Would taking them away from formal schooling set them back irreparably? We worried particularly about Zak, who was just learning to read. The school district reassured us with both advice and books, and Sharon eagerly accepted the position of homeschool teacher for all four boys.

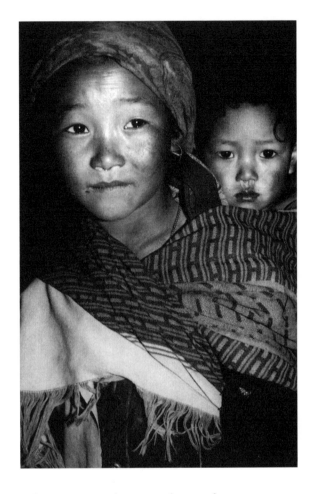

We shipped thousands of dollars in medical supplies ahead of us by plane, the goods donated by various organizations and pharmaceutical companies. We carried our personal items, chosen from a packing list that evolved over months, including schoolbooks, a few clothes, peanut butter, Frisbees, a soccer ball, a deck of cards, toothpaste, and toilet paper. Miscalculating the temperature, we brought warm jackets that sat unused most of the time in favor of simple sweaters. Our hiking boots proved more useful.

We spent ten days in India before arriving in Nepal. For the children, the change from the States proved shocking. The heat stifled.

Sanitary conditions to which they were accustomed appeared nonex-istent. Children, many of them maimed, begged in the streets. How was it possible, questioned my well-fed youngsters, that these children had no house, no food, no mother and father to take care of them?

The poverty we saw in India so affected us that an actual sense of relief accompanied our arrival in Kathmandu, the capital of Nepal. Our welcoming committee consisted of a smiling Nepalese named Bhola who worked for Helping Hands and who was to be our live-in guide, interpreter, and cook for the next five months.

During our month in Kathmandu, we stayed with a Nepalese family that was rather well-off by local standards. The father, an importer, even spoke English. From their home I walked twenty-five minutes to the volunteer clinic each day after breakfast and again after lunch. The clinic was in a rented building and not fully staffed. For the month I was there, the foreign workers consisted of two other American physicians, a nurse practitioner, and a pharmacist from England. Helping Hands provided our food and housing allowance but no pay.

My assignment with Helping Hands included getting this clinic up and running, eventually self-supporting, and staffed by a full-time local doctor. High personnel turnover and the generalized poverty of the people hampered such efforts. In theory, the clinics charge a minimum of a few rupees (the equivalent of fifty cents) for consultation and medicines—enough to support the Nepalese physicians. In truth, few patients can afford to pay anything, so few do.

In the United States, the ratio of population to doctors is fewer than four hundred to one. In Nepal, it runs more than twelve thousand to one. The doctors they do have prefer the cities, leaving rural areas—home to 90 percent of the population—virtually without medical care. The Nepalese government has tried to set up health posts in these areas, assigning recently graduated medical students to train local healthcare workers. These local workers receive no formal medical schooling but apprentice themselves to the doctor and practice hands-on care. They learn the basics, finishing with what we would consider a first-aid level of knowledge. This leaves them capable of handling most of the everyday mishaps and sicknesses they see.

The idea of far-flung clinics staffed by one doctor and various healthcare workers has merit in the case of Nepal. Unfortunately, the government's lack of organization and follow-through defeats its own purpose, and the medical supplies critical to the outposts frequently fail to get beyond Kathmandu. The geography of Nepal proves a major obstacle, as everything taken to rural areas must get there by foot.

After a month in Kathmandu, it was to just such a rural clinic that my family and I traveled. Eight other foreign doctors, three Nepalese doctors, and support staff accompanied us, all organized through Helping Hands. We arrived together at the village of Bandipur to offer a ten-day clinic for the nine hundred or so people from the sur-rounding countryside.

Eighty percent of the Nepalese have worms, so we automatically dewormed all the children we saw. Many of these children showed signs of malnutrition, explaining, in part, why Nepal has one of the highest infant death rates in the world.

One mother, leaving her other children behind in her village, had walked for two days with her baby to reach our clinic to seek a saving miracle. Barefoot in a climate that was comfortable during the day but cold in the evenings, she wore a head wrap and displayed the *bindi*, a red Hindu dot, on her forehead. Many layers of once-bright red, orange, and brown cotton covered her body but not her fear as she handed me her baby. Carefully I unwrapped the rags around the tiny form. Sick and unable to keep down even breast milk, at eighteen months the little boy weighed less than four and a half pounds.

We put the child in the little infirmary next door, administering oral fluids and antibiotics. After eighteen hours, while still lethargic, he had definitely improved. The mother, however, was desperate. She had left her other children with an uncle in her village, and she was worried about them. She wanted to take her sick infant home. Through the interpreter, we argued that we needed to keep the child for three or four weeks, but that she could come and go as necessary. We planned to have the baby live with us and care for him twenty-four hours a day. Reluctantly, after much discussion, the mother acquiesced, and I breathed a sigh of relief. The next morning, however, both mother and child had disappeared.

I considered going to her village and searching for her but was counseled against it. The mother would neither leave her other children nor would she be separated from her baby. I felt helpless. Although I never saw him again, in my heart I feel certain that the baby died.

Death is a familiar visitor in Nepal. Most families I know have lost one or two children. For this reason, among others, they have many children. Parents anticipate the loss of some. The common belief in reincarnation does not make death any easier. It does, however, make it more graciously accepted than in Western cultures. The people in Nepal do not try to hang on to life by prolonging death, as we often do.

Another family brought in a sixteen-year-old who had sustained a severe head injury when he fell out of a tree. Comatose as he was, they fully expected him to die. When, to everyone's surprise, he awoke, we wanted to send him to Kathmandu for follow-up, but the family refused. We kept him at the health post for two to three months. At the end of this time he remained wobbly and not fully in control of his body. During his recovery, the family checked in intermittently. Whether they were simply resigned to his probable death or were anticipating one less mouth to feed, I do not know.

The other doctors and Helping Hands staff members stayed in Bandipur for ten days, during which we all lived in tents. A hole in

the ground served as a latrine, while a makeshift stall offered some privacy. We showered with bags of water heated in the sun, alternating days because of the difficulty of obtaining water. When the other doctors and support workers moved on, my family and I remained another two months, taking up quarters in two rooms of an abandoned schoolhouse.

Americans take for granted the convenience of indoor plumbing and running tap water. Every day, morning and night, Bhola would walk to the center of town where a communal trough held water piped in from the mountains. He filled two brass containers with four to five gallons each and carried the precious liquid home on his shoulders. Normally this is considered women's work, but Bhola accepted the job uncomplainingly, devoted as he was to caring for our family. This water, a total of sixteen to twenty gallons a day, had to serve the six of us and Bhola for baking, drinking, brushing our teeth, and cooking. What we drank, of course, we boiled. We washed clothes rarely.

Showering remained problematic. I stood next to the schoolhouse and never failed to draw a crowd as I stripped to the waist, then washed, brushed my teeth, and cleaned my hair all with a half bucket of water. Sharon, of necessity, bathed inside the school, the water soaking into the dirt floor.

Having finished my work at Bandipur, I moved on to Chainpur, a remote village in eastern Nepal, flying to a grassy strip in the middle of nowhere, then hiking two days further in. My four boys and Bhola accompanied me. Sharon remained behind in Kathmandu to complete the adoption process for a little Nepalese girl who had won our hearts. The old cliché about receiving more than you give took on new meaning for us as we came to Nepal with four children and left with five.

We first encountered eight-year-old Chandra when she and two brothers came to the camp in Bandipur from a village an hour away. She was throwing up and had worms and lice but also a spunky personality. Sharon cleaned her up and outfitted her with a shirt and pants of Zak's. As the days went on, Chandra returned to the camp to visit us. When I inquired about the family, bystanders identified them as orphans, causing me some surprise when I later learned that they had a mother. Their father, it appeared, had indeed died, and their mother didn't count. The low status accorded women in Nepal meant that people considered fatherless children as orphans, whether or not they had a mother.

Chandra took to us and we to her. She hung around, allowing Sharon to keep her clean and enjoying our company and food. The initiative to join our family on a permanent basis came from her and her mother. With two sisters, six brothers, and no father, food was scarce. Chandra readily admits that the quantity of food she received with us affected her decision as much as our affection for her. Furthermore, her mother knew what awaited her in her village. She herself had been married off at eleven, and Chandra's sisters had faced arranged marriages at twelve. One sister was mistreated by her husband; another had died in childbirth. Chandra's own arranged marriage could not lie far in the future.

Neither Chandra nor her mother had, of course, any concept of the distance, either geographically or culturally, between Nepal and the United States, and thought that she could go back and forth at will. They assumed that life must be much the same (after all, we slept on the floor as they did), except that we had warm sleeping bags and enough food. Chandra's mother, illiterate, held aspirations for her daughter to attend school. Life with us offered a brighter future.

So it was that Sharon stayed behind to battle Nepalese red tape while I went ahead with our four boys and Bhola. (Innocent as we

were, we did not realize until after the fact that the government officials whose foot-dragging disrupted our family unity were simply
waiting for bribes to expedite the adoptive process.)

At the remote health post in Chainpur where we stayed for seven
weeks, the Nepalese physician departed when I arrived, leaving only
the two health aides to work with me. Of necessity, I drafted Bhola
and an interpreter from the village to help with the patients who
walked in. Twice a week, we hiked to different schools in the sur-
rounding mountains to give health education lessons. Cover up your
feces. Don't defecate or urinate near a water source. Boil what you
drink. Keep animals out of the house. We handed out soap and toothbrushes to be kept in the school and used as part of each day's routine.
This health education was probably worth more in the long run than
the medicines I dispensed at the clinic.

We stayed in a local house owned by an elderly couple who
reserved the two second-floor rooms for themselves while renting out
the dirt-floor ground level to us. Bhola, an experienced cook who had
accompanied expeditions to a Mt. Everest base camp, used a one-
burner kerosene stove to make rice and *daal,* a lentil soup to pour over
the rice. We also ate oatmeal and *chapatis* (flour tortillas) on which we
spread our rationed peanut butter. Milk, mainly from goats or water
buffalo, did not form part of our regular diet. On the rare occasions
when one of our interpreters brought some, we boiled the unpasteur-
ized product, then rationed it out in a watered-down version of milk
tea with sugar. We also had occasional meat when Bhola was able to
purchase a live chicken or goat to kill and prepare.

Most Nepalese eat only two meals a day, rice and *daal* both times.
Knowing we were used to more, Bhola worried about us, especially the
children. We were well into our stay in Nepal before we realized that
the good man was actually supplementing our diet with part of his

minimal Helping Hands salary because our food allowance was not enough. Needless to say, we repaid him as soon as we found out.

His strong work ethic and genuine concern for us made him reluctant to take a day off. On one occasion when Sharon had finally insisted he take a break, he returned the next day to bewail the stale bread and old bananas she had been sold without his bartering skills. He insisted that he be the one to do the shopping in the future. His willingness—even eagerness—to work stood in stark contrast to many of the men, especially in rural areas. There we commonly saw the men out gambling in the street while the women, babies on their backs, worked the fields. Those with whom Sharon talked could not comprehend her happiness at having our family together. They could imagine nothing nicer than having a husband who worked so hard that he was gone for hours each day.

Three years later, our family, complete with Chandra, returned to Nepal for three and a half months. The ever-faithful Bhola, who freelanced his services to several organizations, accompanied us once more. This time, we worked under the auspices of the Himalayan Rescue Association, an organization founded by an American but currently run by Nepalese, to treat altitude sickness. Its outposts sit among the mountains at Pheriche (fourteen thousand feet) and Menang (twelve thousand feet). There the air is thin, and the effects of overexertion and rapid change of altitude can be deadly. Nausea, headache, fatigue, and shortness of breath present themselves as dire warning symptoms. The trekker who does not heed them exposes himself or herself to possible pulmonary or cerebral edema, fatal if not treated.

We stayed in Menang, a seven-day hike from the nearest road and four days away from an eighteen-thousand-foot pass into the next valley. Of the indigenous sufferers we saw, most were porters hired to carry goods or packs for trekkers. As their salaries depended on how much they could carry and how fast, they occasionally overexerted themselves and failed to take sufficient time to adjust when moving to a higher altitude.

We chose preventive education as our main tactic, at the same time treating the cases presented to us. Restraining the patient from ascending any further cured mild altitude sickness until he or she had adjusted. Sometimes we sent trekkers to a lower altitude. In more serious cases, we put patients inside a Gamow bag, a rubber cylinder pressurized by a foot pump to simulate lowering the altitude by three thousand feet. For the severely ill, once a day—the only time we could get through—we could contact Kathmandu by radio to request a helicopter evacuation. This service, organized by foreign embassies, served foreigners only. A severely ill Nepalese would have to be transported out by ambulance. Since Menang lay a seven-day hike from the nearest road, this possibility existed more in theory than in reality. Fortunately, most of the victims I saw were foreigners. The majority of Nepalese presented more mundane complaints similar to those I had seen on our earlier trip.

Menang's population was mainly Tibetan, the religion Buddhist rather than Hindu. Above Menang, up a thousand feet of winding path, we made the acquaintance of an elderly lama and his wife, dwellers in a mountain cave. Over eighty years old, the couple kept themselves warm by the heat of a fire and lived off potatoes they buried in the cave floor so they wouldn't freeze in the winter. Our children would hike up and offer them much-appreciated coffee and vegetables. In return, the woman would serve a meal of tea and boiled potatoes. Shared food and smiles substituted for language. In our home, we keep a large framed photo of this couple and our five children.

This elderly lama and his wife had pulled away from the rest of society in order to lead a life of solitude and contemplation. Yet it amazed me how much even the rest of the population, moving about their everyday chores, considered religion an integral rather than separate facet of their existence. Omnipresent prayer flags and prayer wheels offered constant opportunities for prayer. People wore prayer beads as a matter of course. They respected all life and exuded compassion, gentleness, peacefulness, and concern for others. They led Christlike lives without professing Christianity. Our culture could learn from them that religion is not just a Sunday event.

I would like to return to Nepal to see Chandra's family and the many friends we have there now. Yes, the rural buildings are only mud stucco, cold and dark, explaining why people prefer to be outdoors and why they carry patients on pallets to lie in the sun during the day. There is no running water or sanitation, and eating conditions remain rustic.

Yet Sharon and I both think back on how peaceful our life was there. With neither the conveniences nor the distractions of modern technology, we walked everywhere, rested, and shared family time by playing card games and soccer. We slept together in a pile in a single room on a dirt floor, and everyone slept well. The phone never rang because there wasn't one.

We learned about the Nepalese. They learned about us. Around Christmas on our first trip, our children and Bhola's put on a Nativity play under Sharon's direction. As the interpreters explained the circumstances and rendered the story into Nepalese, the onlookers expressed surprise that our god came from a humble setting like the one in which they lived, unlike the powerful, glamorous origins of their gods. Even Bhola, knowing us as he did, admitted that for the first time he understood why we had wanted Chandra, whose low-caste origins made her unattractive to most in her country.

I would return to Nepal, but I would also like to travel elsewhere to volunteer. No matter where I go, I can apply the most important—and ironic—lesson I learned. I went to Nepal hoping to repay the debt I owed humanity by providing medical care that would make a difference. Once there, I realized that while I did indeed make a difference for individual people on a short-term basis, a long-term improvement is possible only through a change in basic living conditions. Since Nepalese adults seemed little interested in change, we focused on the children by teaching in schools and clinics. With time, it is this education—not my medical skills—that will lighten the obligation I feel.

Thailand

Operation Smile

Better Than Not Catching Fish

"I wouldn't say I'm called to do this. I'm not that noble.
But if I'm a healthy adult with some usable skills, why not share?"

PAT HEPNER

REGISTERED NURSE

In many parts of the world, children born with defects do not receive the surgeries they would in the United States. They grow into adulthood with disfigurations of one kind or another that reduce their chances for a good job, a normal circle of friends, or even a future marriage and family. Operation Smile sends plastic surgeons into these countries where, for months in advance, local public and private social services have been making a list of the patients they consider likely to benefit from reconstructive surgery. The organization specializes in cleft palate and cleft lip deformities, always with the goal of returning to the same location two years in a row, so that a child who has both problems can have one repaired on each occasion. Doctors also correct terrible scarring left from burns, a not uncommon occurrence in areas where the source for both cooking and heat is an open fire.

For the first day or two, a team screens all those who show up. Some have come from very far, walking, riding a donkey or horse, or traveling by bus. They stand in line beginning at sunup. Doctors triage them into definite candidates for surgery, second priorities, and maybes. Once operations start, they take place every forty-five minutes from seven in the morning until eight at night.

With Operation Smile, in contrast to my wound clinic job in the States, I worked in pre- and post-op. I prepared the children, then took care of them for two or three days after their surgeries. Other differences concerned the facilities, equipment, and staff. The hospital we used in Venezuela actually had air-conditioned surgical suites, although parts of the building lacked running water.

In developing countries, instruments don't go off to the autoclave for sterilization as they do here. Due to the limited number of instruments available, we used a system of front table (clean instruments) and back table (instruments soaking in disinfectant after being cleaned with soap, water, and a toothbrush). We reused surgical drapes as well. Cloths for the surgical field were cut to size and used sparingly. Taking such care with limited medical resources led my thoughts to our resources in general. We waste so much in America. Yet, within the medical field, regulatory agencies will allow no less, as they expect perfection to the nth degree.

As I prepared for my Fairview-sponsored Thailand trip in 1999, I thought back to my Operation Smile experience in Venezuela two years earlier. In the government hospital in the city of Barcelona, the nurses wore high heels and starched white uniforms. They sat in little offices and barked occasional orders to overworked aides but did little themselves. Patient rooms contained three items: a bed, a mattress, and a chair. No sheets. No towels. No toilet paper. No throw-up basin. No pillow. No blanket. No wastebasket or bedpan. Should one of the children vomit, the mother could go down several flights to the commissary and buy paper towels with which to clean it up.

Bugs crawled everywhere on the beds, on the walls, on the floors. The water cut off at noon. The local nurses would steal our things, so we had to carry our medical supplies with us at all times. The hospital allowed us the fourth floor for surgery and the eighth floor for postoperative recovery. There was no elevator. We started at 7:30 A.M., and by 10:00 A.M. I was drenched in sweat. "I am really nuts," I thought to myself as my tired arms carried the umpteenth child from the fourth floor to the eighth, my leaden legs becoming heavier with each successive step. "I must be a crazy person. Could I please go home now?"

I got over the shock in the first couple of days. With the passage of time, as women who have borne children know, one forgets how bad it was and remembers instead the result. As an example, I recall a teenage boy with a cleft lip and palate and a twinkle in his eye who demonstrated none of the meekness and reticence so common to these people. He wanted both surgeries at once, despite our objections that one would be better this year, the other the next. Undeterred, he hung around, making himself useful any way he could, deliberately endearing himself to all of us. His perseverance earned him the double surgery.

I had anticipated the difference in ambiance between South America and Southeast Asia. In heavily Buddhist Thailand, orange-robed monks with bald heads lined the road every day at sunrise to receive food from middle class families on their way to work. A large proportion of the population supported these contemplative monks, giving them donations of rice, vegetables, and fruits in plastic bags which the monks received in what appeared to be stainless steel mixing bowls. Buddhist temples stood everywhere, some of them in a continual state of renovation.

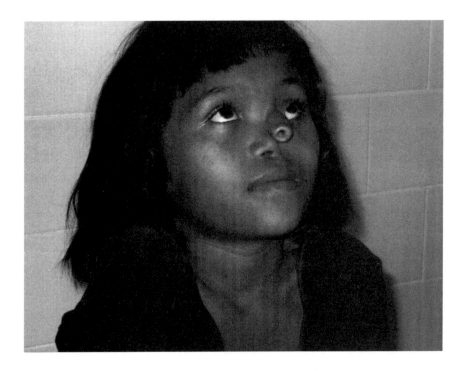

We worked in the town of Yasothon, about five hundred miles northeast of Bangkok, close to the Laotian border and the Mekong River. The biggest town (I would guess twenty thousand people) in this largely agricultural area, Yasothon correlated to a county seat and was home to the only hospital for many miles. People came from the area around, impressing us with their friendliness and warmth.

Amway, distributor of cleaning products and volunteer sponsor of Operation Smile, provided us with bilingual volunteers from its regional corporate headquarters in Bangkok. These eager aides told us when children needed to have their IVs changed, when they needed help, and when they were crying. They functioned as nursing assistants without the title, and their help proved invaluable.

I had not expected the vast improvement in facilities and nurses in Thailand as compared to Venezuela. The staff really cared about the patients and was eager to be of assistance. The hospital had an elevator that sometimes worked and, believe it or not, hot water.

As well as children, we treated older people who had never had reconstructive surgery. In many cases, it proved more emotional to offer this help to an adult than to a child. Some of these people had suffered years of ostracism in their villages because they drooled or their big teeth hung out due to their deformity. Teenagers had no chance of finding a girlfriend or boyfriend. After the operation, they had not only normal looks but the prospect of a fuller life ahead of them.

A young man brought in his older sister who was in her thirties. Frightened and shy, she nearly had to be carried in. You could see her mentally digging in her heels in an attempt to remain outside. She was so shy that it took her several days after the operation to finally smile.

A thirty-three-year-old man walked in, tall and good-looking except for the hairy nevus (a large, hairy mole) that surrounded one eye and came halfway down his cheek. We removed this tennis-ball-sized dermatological malignancy, undoubtedly leaving some scarring but probably saving his life.

People have asked me who should go on these trips. I tell them: anyone who can be flexible. And please, I add, don't be an ugly American. Although we don't go with the specific purpose of representing America, we do it nevertheless. It is unavoidable. I have seen too many rude Americans, those with the "why can't this be like in the United States?" attitude. Things aren't going to be as they are at home. Elevators may not work; air conditioners may not cool; water may not run. Food, definitely, will not be what you're used to. I have seen local stews containing what I thought were eyeballs. I have unknowingly eaten something looking like a canned green pea that was so hot it was unbelievable. I remained polite. "It's a little hot for me," I said with a smile as I reached for the grapes and bananas.

In the time since my trip to Thailand, Operation Smile has reviewed and revised its policies. It now allows only pediatric medical care workers. Pediatrics not being my specialty, I no longer qualify as a team participant. Instead, I am looking into making future trips with groups that do club foot or other repairs. I work with a couple of orthopedists who think I would do just fine.

Why would I rather do this than take a week at a northern cabin and go fishing? This proves more exciting than a regular vacation and more worthwhile. I learn a lot while I help other people. I wouldn't say I'm *called* to do this. I'm not that noble. But if I'm a healthy adult with some usable skills, why not share? Besides, I get tired of not catching fish.

When my husband and I retire, we may live in a foreign country and work there for a couple of years with the Peace Corps or a similar organization. We both believe in this. There is so much to do.

GUATEMALA

Operation Guatemala

Rejoicing in What They Have

"Death is an accepted part of everyday life."

DANIEL DEBBAN

NURSE ANESTHETIST

Operation Guatemala, active since the early 1990s, grew out of Wooddale Community Church in Eden Prairie, Minnesota. Originally begun by American missionaries, Operation Guatemala now incorporates medical missions as well as evangelical. In 1999, a dozen people from my church accepted Wooddale's invitation to join them on a trip to the Central American nation. I just happened to be sitting in church on the right Sunday, saw the slide presentation, filled out an application on the spur of the moment, and was accepted.

Each team member collected between seventeen and eighteen hundred dollars—not that much for me, but perhaps one or two years' salary for a Guatemalan. We also took medicines and clothing, leaving nearly all behind us and returning with little. I brought my own sutures, scissors, and forceps, items used only once by American hospitals and then tossed. These little contributions proved well appreciated in Guatemala, where even a hospital like the one in Santiago offers

1960s vintage equipment. The main hospital in Guatemala City owns a total of six ventilators. What do they do, I asked, if they need another? A nurse will "hand bag" the patient, I was told (manually squeeze oxygen, one squeeze for each breath), until one becomes available.

We based our team near Atitlán, Guatemala's large volcanic lake. From there we traveled out to smaller villages where we would construct homes, teach people to build solar ovens, and pass out vitamins and deworming medicines as well as antibiotics if a doctor accompanied the group. Despite governmental efforts, I found rural villages lacking in both medical care and continuity. Government teams came once a year with antiparasitic medicine, but under the conditions with which they lived, the people were quickly reinfected, as evidenced by the number of children with oversized bellies.

One side of the lake seemed relatively modern. The other side, where we worked, boasted a nice church built by Americans but only huts for the villagers and no toilet facilities. We used a respectable quantity of bug spray to discourage the flies. The natives, many suffering from lice, ringworm, and various ulcerations due to a lack of hygiene, entered with flies swarming around them and left amid the same swarm, like the Li'l Abner character forever accompanied by his personal rain cloud. We tried to teach basic hygiene—such simple things as washing and bathing—while realizing the difficulty of carrying these out without the proper facilities.

Death is an accepted part of everyday life in Guatemala. We came upon a little cemetery with numerous small graves, two or three feet long. A man we asked lifted his shoulders with a "nothing-out-of-the-ordinary" shrug. "They had a big sickness. A lot of children died."

We hesitated to dispense too many antibiotics, even with a doctor present. The people had only a minimal education. Would they follow our instructions on dose and length of medication? Would they take too much at once in the belief that more was better? Would they take one pill and hoard the rest for future use, thereby invalidating the medication's effectiveness and building up resistance to its effect in the future?

While her husband worked in the fields, a mother in her early teens brought in a three-year-old boy whose size would have put him at half that age. Born with congenital cataracts, a heart murmur, and a skin condition that left ulcerations over his entire body, the little one looked up from his mother's arms through eyes that could barely see. A shawl covered some of the ulcers on his head. Pants and a shirt hid those on his body. Those on his bare feet remained exposed. He must have been used to the pain, as he didn't whimper or cry. Instead, he reached out his hand to touch mine as his eyes detected my movement.

I marveled at how that mother loved her child, at the extra care she must have given to keep him alive this long. He had done as well as could be expected of any child in the United States under similar adverse conditions. His mother, for obvious reasons, feared having another child. We offered words of encouragement and antiparasitic medicines. There was no point in giving antibiotics; the boy had no hope. In a few weeks, he would be gone. Not a dry eye remained in the room as that mother carried her little one out.

My group traveled up into the mountains to do some rebuilding. I served as nurse for the five of us Americans and the five Guatemalans who accompanied us (all of whom gave up a week of pay to do so). The minimal medicines we brought covered the expected cases of sunburn, blisters, back strain, and dehydration. I also carried medicine for anaphylactic shock (allergic reaction to bee stings), just in case.

Our guides directed us to a simple church, still standing but partially destroyed and unsafe after an earthquake two decades ago. Along with the local people, we rebuilt that rudimentary church, enjoying the satisfaction of seeing villagers hold their first service there in twenty-two years.

The missionary group that formed our in-country contact had taken care of all the trip logistics, including housing and transportation. Conditions, as expected, proved rustic, but I didn't mind sleeping on cement or dirt in a sleeping bag. We brought nonperishable hiking-type food but ended up staying at the home of one of the better-off villagers, where $20 a day bought all of us three meals and lodging.

With the exception of the first day, in which I ingested cow's hoof soup that made me sick, conditions proved adequate. We ate a lot of chicken, rice, beans, and tortillas, and drank bottled water only. We washed our hands with the alcohol wash we brought, as the local water left something to be desired, and considered the food safe if it was cooked and still hot. Evenings we wandered to the local stream, stripped to our shorts, and bathed while giggling kids enjoyed the spectacle from the bridge above.

I would qualify rural Guatemala as a beautiful setting that hosted a lot of sickness because of inadequate sanitation facilities. I think back to that large church built by an American group on the side of the lake where we started out. It even had electricity! Wouldn't that group have done better to build the villagers a shower facility?

Many organizations help Guatemala. I know that others will continue where ours left off. Nevertheless, we lack coordination. Different churches do different things. How much more could we do if we each knew what the other was doing, if we coordinated and worked together. There remains, of course, the debatable question of which is better, to treat numerous people for worms or a few selected individuals with serious operable conditions. There are organizations for each.

When I near retirement (I'm fifty-nine now), I plan to learn Spanish to enhance my communication with villagers. I'll go more

often to share the talents I have. Nurse anesthesia is difficult in many areas because of the lack of equipment, but there remains so much more I can do.

I wouldn't go on my own. Only naiveté would encourage one to jump in alone without the backing and protection of an organization. We heard local talk of guerrilla activity and kidnappings, but never actually saw anything more threatening than a fight down a side street. Nevertheless, we traveled in groups of two or more, and on one occasion I found myself appropriately scolded for wandering off to take pictures. We wore our Operation Guatemala shirts at all times. This device not only got us through customs without the necessity of a bribe, but informed all that we didn't come as rich tourists.

I wore steel-toed boots. By the partially rebuilt church, I stood my foot next to that of a man whose worn shoes hadn't long to last, noting that we wore about the same size. When I left, I gave him my steel-toed boots, for him a prized possession. We also donated all the clothing we didn't need to wear as well as pamphlets on first aid and basic hygiene.

The people I met don't have an easy life, yet they seem happy. We have so much in the States, yet we complain. Guatemalan villagers live from day to day, keeping their families alive. Many have no running water, electricity, or available healthcare. For them, labor remains largely physical and backbreaking. Men plow the fields by hand for planting; women carry stacks of firewood for cooking; pack horses bring loads of river stones for building. Yet these diminutive people don't consider themselves poor, as they rejoice in what they have.

Guatemalans remain overtly friendly. In one village, we received a bag of oranges as a thank-you. As I walked down the road, I passed a young mother with a crying toddler. I put an orange in his little hand, at which he stopped his crying and smiled. The whole trip was worth it for that smile.

I plan to go back again if there is an opportunity. What's more, I'll make the opportunity.

Nigeria

Pro Health International

The Joy of Caring

"I have no supplies.
I have the manpower and the training, but nothing to use."

SHIRLEY GRAF
REGISTERED NURSE

Every year, like a New Year's resolution, I reset my priorities. I remind myself not to take my blessings, including the clean, running water in my faucet, for granted. I stop complaining if the electricity goes out for five minutes. Most of the places to which Pro Health International goes in Nigeria have no running water at all and produce electricity only with the help of a generator.

This nongovernmental, nondenominational Christian organization delivers healthcare to rural villages in West Africa. I have been a participant since 1995. This last time, I traveled to Africa alone, flying from Minneapolis to Amsterdam to Lagos, Nigeria, where I stayed in a local hotel. The next day I flew to the town of Jos, the home of the doctor in charge of Pro Health for Nigeria. From there, I rode the bus for hours to the village where I would stay a week with other volunteers, mostly Nigerian doctors and nurses who spoke English.

Our house for the week consisted of one large room used for eating and meeting and four smaller ones in which we slept on a bed, a mattress, or the floor, depending on availability. We used the liberal supply of buckets filled with water for outdoor cooking and for pouring down toilets that had no other means of flushing.

The second week we traveled to a different village and stayed in the local hotel, a complex made up of what appeared to be small houses. Ours had eight rooms in which three people shared a room with the necessary buckets of water and a stock of bottled drinking water. The third week we actually stayed in a modern hotel outside Abuja, the capital city, enjoying the comfort of running water and taking the bus every day to a village.

Each time I travel to Africa, my diet consists of oatmeal for breakfast, a peanut butter sandwich for lunch, and rice or pasta for supper.

Due to recommendations from my travel clinics, I never eat meat in Africa. The villagers serve it for supper, eating a combination of pounded yams, fish, a meat sauce or soup, and *gerry*, a mush eaten with the fingers and dipped in the sauce or soup. Their breakfasts don't differ much from mine, consisting of oatmeal, eggs, bread, and sometimes the equivalent of our pork and beans. A sandwich makes up their lunch meal. People tend to eat a lot because the intestinal worms that most of them carry absorb much of their caloric intake.

In Africa, I have never encountered any animosity toward America, or anything, for that matter, other than great respect. People demonstrate an interest in our lives, wanting to know what our typical day is like or how an American hospital functions. The week before I arrived in Jos, the town had experienced uprisings between Christians and Muslims. I walked through an airport in which a group of people knelt on prayer rugs and prayed the 5:00 P.M. prayer to Allah, and I never felt unsafe. Pro Health treats both Christians and Muslims.

Respect for Americans extends beyond Nigeria. I spent a week as a tourist in Egypt just after the 2001 World Trade Center attack. The amount of support for our country surprised me. People in both Egypt and Nigeria couldn't understand how it took us so long to do something about Osama bin Laden. Their countrymen also died on September 11.

Nigeria has no middle class; people are rich or poor. The rich frequently have connections with the corrupt government and have access to medical care in private hospitals. The poor, on the other hand, are relegated to government hospitals totally lacking in supplies and offering operating rooms that you have to clean before you would even think of operating there. In one such hospital, not a single surgical procedure had taken place in the last six months due to a lack of doctors.

Had doctors been available, the lack of any supplies would have prohibited operations anyway. When we go, we bring everything—sutures, tapes, scalpels—knowing that we can count on nothing locally. A Nigerian doctor, lamenting the state of medical care in his country, told me, "I have no supplies. I have the manpower and the training, but nothing to use."

I become so motivated when I see all the things we have here that Nigerian doctors and hospitals need—not only supplies but medicines. Ancef, for example—the antibiotic given as a prophylactic to surgery patients—costs as little as a dollar a dose in the States. In Nigeria, because of the scarcity, you pay $15 for the same amount. Last year I sent two forty-foot containers of medical supplies and medicines. I spent part of the time during my visit assessing the organization and use of these items. Our medical supplies tend to be more sophisticated than what Nigerian doctors are used to, so I teach them ways to use our products.

A significant argument in favor of medical missions centers around the delivery of care to the poor and underserved in developing countries. They suffer from diseases and deformities that go untreated because of cost and the lack of hospitals. Medical problems we consider simple here have become major there. We see individuals with polio, rickets, and self-set broken bones. I have seen women with benign uterine fibroids so large that the women look nine months pregnant when they lie down on the table. I have seen breast cancers with draining abscesses and absolutely no treatment. In the United States, a hernia that doctors consider "large" may have reached the size of a lemon. In Nigeria, I have seen hernias the size of a basketball. Hernias here are repaired in a few months, but in Nigeria they go five, ten, fifteen years with no medical attention. I have seen a thirty-year-old woman with horribly enlarged and leathered legs, the result of untreated elephantiasis caused by a parasitic worm. Readily treatable in the early stages by a simple prescription, her untreated disease had progressed to the point where she would eventually have to have her legs amputated. Yet these African people accept their lot and do not complain. They consistently prove grateful for anything we can do for them and have taught me so much about gratitude.

We perform surgeries in village health centers (basically any room big enough) functioning something like a MASH unit. With no sterilizers, we soak instruments in disinfectant for twelve minutes before reusing them. Up to seven patients may lie in beds in the same room where we do surgeries. We use local anesthetic, sedation, and spinal anesthesia, as I have yet to see an anesthesia machine in Nigeria that looks reliable enough to trust.

I realize that we help only a few people among the thousands who need it, but I have never doubted the worth of our work even for these few. I have resuscitated a newborn baby. I have seen a fourteen-year-old boy blind from cataracts dance for joy after we removed one; now he could see and go to school. We repaired the hernia of a man who had saved as much as he could from his harvests for the past three years while the hernia continued to worsen. He still had not accumulated what he would have needed for a government hospital operation. Another man, crippled by a bone disease, walked in on his knees, the same way he planted and harvested his crops. His native African robe had been shortened from the height of a normal man to allow him to move in this manner. We fixed his hernia also and watched him walk out on his knees, no doubt in some pain but never complaining. Joy shone on his face at having had one of his problems resolved.

In the United States, the medical field is buried in paperwork. In Nigeria, I never touch a piece of paper. I just do the work and experience the sheer joy of caring.

I educate, too, inasmuch as local possibilities allow for improvements. I used to see people exposed to blood because they worked barefoot during surgery. Now, many wear tennis shoes as well as goggles. Out of necessity, they wash and reuse supplies, including the surgical gowns, because they can't get more. They disinfect needles and use them again because they don't have enough new ones to go around.

I have learned to retain an open mind and not be judgmental of the way Nigerians do things. How can you criticize people who have no other choice?

Haiti

Project Haiti

Forgotten Country

*"Just the fact that you show up there
is very much appreciated by the local people."*

STEVEN MOORE

UROLOGIST

The Pignon hospital was low on morphine, and the tremendous postoperative pain suffered by twenty-three-year-old Gina Benoit distressed me as I worked on other patients and checked in on her. Typically thin—you don't see many overweight Haitians—this patient carried her Bible with her, perhaps as a comfort in a situation frightening to most, especially to one who didn't speak the doctor's language and communicated only through an interpreter. From birth, her body had worked on a single kidney. I operated and removed the obstruction in her left kidney, leaving her with two healthy organs.

Fellow surgeon Paul Severson, who had traveled to Pignon for ten years, first introduced me to Project Haiti, a secular organization affiliated with the Christian Mission of Pignon. A town of some five thousand people, Pignon lies in the northern section of Haiti, south of the larger city of Cap-Haïtien. The hospital in Pignon runs under the direction of Dr. Guy Theodore, a Haitian with medical training from the States. Unlike many who want to stay out once they have had the good fortune to get out, Dr. Theodore returned to his native land determined to raise hospital standards and do what he could for his people. Project Haiti, composed mostly of surgeons but also of orthopedists, anesthesiologists, family practitioners, nurses, and nonmedical personnel who distribute food, takes teams to the Pignon hospital to perform the surgeries for which doctors are unavailable. Our team had twelve people.

You have to be prepared to work in filthy conditions when you go on a mission like this. Noise fills the night. If you turn on your flashlight to go to the bathroom in the dark, startled mice and insects scurry away. Animals survive—or don't—in the streets. You live in primitive conditions. If you can't part with the luxuries and amenities of home for a week, don't go. If, however, you can put up with temporary discomfort, the rewards of such a mission are nothing less than outstanding.

I had never traveled to a developing country until my first trip with Project Haiti. My initial impression can only be termed as shock, not only at the abject poverty that was there, but at the lack of things that weren't—sanitary public services, roads, transportation, and electricity. Much of Haiti has no electricity at all. Existing roads rate "horrible," as demonstrated by the thirty-five mountainous miles we covered in—believe it or not—four hours. Malnourished children with swollen bellies crowd into shacks in this heavily populated country. You feel like you have taken a step back into another world of a century ago.

The Haitian government contributes some funding to the Pignon hospital, as does Dr. Theodore, who has used much of his own money to help. The second floor, reserved for wealthy people, consists of suites with only one or two patients per room. These patients come mostly from Port-au-Prince, the reputation of the American doctors having drawn them to the Pignon hospital. The money these wealthy patients pay keeps the hospital going for the poor, who only pay what they can to the permanent Haitian staff and nothing to the temporary American doctors.

Our team stayed in the dormitory on the grounds next to the hospital, where we enjoyed the comfort of indoor plumbing and electricity run by a generator during the day. At night when the generator was turned off we used flashlights and slept four to six in a room with cots. In the dormitory dining room we ate three clean meals a day prepared by cooks that Dr. Theodore provided. We remained leery of the well water, which can carry bacterial diseases, and limited ourselves to bottled drinking water.

In addition to the generally wretched conditions of the populace, I was appalled by the extent to which many suffered remediable diseases or physical abnormalities for lack of medical intervention. I witnessed things I had never seen, even in a textbook. A woman came in with a sarcoma the size of a grapefruit on the bridge of her nose. The senses resist believing that such things are possible, yet there they are, staring you in the face. A team doctor removed the sarcoma, leaving the woman with a face that looked human again and a potentially greater life span.

A mother brought in a one-year-old girl with a large abdominal mass. With nothing more than crude X-rays to guide us, we remained unsure of what we were dealing with until we opened her up. One of the team doctors performed the surgery, doing an excellent job of removing the tumor from one of the infant's kidneys. Since the hospital had no pathology department, we sent the tumor to Port-au-Prince for analysis. A determination that would have taken two or three days in the States took that many weeks in Haiti. We had left by the time the results came back.

The hospital—substandard by any American criterion—was perhaps thirty years old, cramped, run-down, and dirty. Like our dorm, it did offer running water and toilets and generator-run electricity during the day. The lower floor contained some fifty beds. Physical and financial restrictions dictated that eight or ten patients be crowded into a room measuring ten by thirty feet. The hospital provided no meals and only limited nursing services, so the patients' families brought them food, washed them, and helped them to the toilet. Family members often slept on the floor under the patient's bed in order to care for him or her at night. Nurses administered medication.

Anesthesiology equipment desperately needed updating, as it repeatedly broke down due to age. In the second of two operating rooms, the oxygen tank didn't work well, and the general anesthesia equipment wouldn't function at all, leaving local or spinal anesthetics the only possibilities. There was no intravenous equipment, no machinery to monitor the patient or administer gases.

Aware of this lack, we brought what we could. I brought the surgical supplies I knew I would use. A fellow doctor brought his own laparoscopic equipment to make possible these procedures. Since Dr. Theodore had picked the patients beforehand, we were able to perform a good number of surgeries that would not have been available were it not for our equipment and training. The Pignon hospital, for example, has no urologist of its own. When I go, I'm it, and I take care of the backlog of untreated patients needing urological surgery. The case of Gina Benoit was only one. In a single trip, I made a difference in the lives of ten patients, including several older men in need of prostate surgery.

Why could I do only ten operations in a week? The reasons are both physical and cultural. Lack of equipment proved an obvious stumbling block. A lab test that would take an hour here took a day or more

in Pignon. Among the Haitian medical staff, I generally did not find the same sense of urgency to get things done that one expects in the United States. Many of the Haitian people didn't have a clear understanding of how to run a hospital, but we had to work with them. Case turnover became a lengthy process. From the patient standpoint, communication posed a problem. The language gap was obvious, the cultural less so. Most had limited education, making it difficult for them to understand what they needed, what I was going to do, and what they had to do as follow-up.

Cultural differences and those of value systems prove difficult to overcome. For example, the concept of marriage differs from our institution here. In Haiti, a typical man has a common-law wife as well as other women with whom he has children. This creates a dysfunctional society with multiple health-related issues. Trying to change the

Haitians' generally accepted idea of marriage would be to beat one's head against a wall. Instead, we appeal to their greater sense of wanting to be physically healthy.

Women commonly hold the belief that they should not nurse their babies for the first three days of life in order to trigger a hunger instinct, which encourages the babies to nurse more. Convincing them that this is unhealthy for their babies proves an uphill fight. Likewise, it proves a difficult task to convince them that invisible bacteria in the water of a dirty stream are what give their babies dysentery and cause many of them to die. To remedy the water situation, the Christian Mission of Pignon is routing a mountain spring into a channel for drinking.

I cared about these people, in particular the ones with whom I had some personal interaction. Several months after I returned home, I e-mailed Dr. Theodore asking about Gina Benoit and the little girl. Gina, I was told, had recovered completely and was attending college, happy, healthy, and with the possibility of a normal life ahead of her. The pathological results on the mass we had removed from the little girl had indicated a Wilms' tumor, a particularly aggressive cancer. Nevertheless, with follow-up chemotherapy and radiation, her statistical chances of a cure would have stood at 75 percent. Sadly, such therapy was unavailable. The child had died.

Ninety-five percent of Haitians are of African descent. The rate of HIV/AIDS in Haiti stands at about one-fourth of South Africa's. Yet the fact that many people believe AIDS runs as rampant in Haiti as in parts of Africa has caused a drop in the tourist industry and a resulting rise in poverty.

Haiti is a forgotten country. Just the fact that you show up there is very much appreciated by the local people, whom I found warm and friendly. On my first trip, I made friends in the community to such an extent that I wanted to return to visit them. The hospital needed a urologist again, providing me the perfect impetus.

As a physician in the wealthiest country in the world, I know how privileged I am. I am able to live here, have this career, and share with the less fortunate. In truth, after each trip, I feel more blessed and rewarded than the people I serve. The Haitians have no money, but I have been paid with a shirt or a piece of pottery—this by people who own little more than their pride. Those who have nothing are profuse in their thanks, profound in their gratefulness, always gracious, friendly, and humble.

I come away with a strong sense of appreciation for the Haitian people and how much they struggle. I marvel at how psychologically and spiritually healthy they remain despite their extreme poverty. Each trip, I become a part of the life these people face day by day. I find the experience both ennobling and humbling.

Guatemala

Edinbrook Church

Of Seminaries and Superlatives

"This has made me see how much you can do without,
as well as how much you can accomplish with little."

NANCY HEDLUND
SURGICAL TECHNICIAN

Why, someone asked me, would you spend your vacation offering crude medical clinics in Guatemala instead of lying out on the beach?

Crude they are. Our nine-member team worked in a ten-by-twelve-foot cement room—walls, floor, and ceiling painted a peachy orange—that formed part of the Berea Bible Institute in Huehuetenango, five hours into the mountains northwest of Guatemala City.

The Institute serves as a four-year nondenominational seminary for rural pastors. Coming from surrounding areas to study and board for six months, they return to their far-flung communities to help with the planting season and see their families for the other half of each year. Their previous education equates to our high school. These seminarians are training for a career in which they may earn a little money from their local church, or they may get paid in chickens and other edibles. So that they can survive, along with theology they study baking, carpentry, first aid, or gardening to have a marketable skill. As the Institute charges little because its students have little, it sells the bakery products to subsidize tuition.

Edwin Martínez, our in-country contact and former native of Huehuetenango, is in the process of building a guest house to house groups like ours that work in the area. We ourselves worked on the project when we were not offering clinic hours. Because the house remained unfinished, we stayed in a hotel in town, sharing a hallway bathroom. Each room offered two single beds, cement walls and floor with a small rug, a night table, and, at least in ours, a single unopenable window. There was no fan. Fortunately, while temperatures climbed during the day, it cooled down at night, so we survived. Sometimes we had running water in the form of a trickle or spray from the shower; sometimes we didn't. The price, however, was good: $5 per night.

We ate at the home of an elementary school principal, a friend of our contact. His sister came from Guatemala City and cooked all of our meals for us, assuring us that the vegetables and fruits were washed in Clorox and that only bottled water went into the drinks.

A doctor from Huehuetenango had volunteered during most of the year to diagnose seminary students' ailments and prescribe medicine. Only when we came, however, did free care become available to the general public. So it was that our little medical room saw not only seminarians, but villagers who had walked great distances to reach us. Each day, they lined up and stood waiting when we arrived. Grandparents brought grandchildren; young mothers carried babies; children supported ailing parents. Ages ranged from two months to seventy-nine years.

Edwin, who served as our interpreter, gave out numbers to preserve a semblance of order, and patients entered one at a time. We determined their primary complaint, finding intestinal parasites a common problem. We also diagnosed a lot of vitamin A deficiency and handed out innumerable children's vitamins containing supplements of this necessary nutrient. The people in general ate a daily diet of tortillas, beans, rice, and a little meat but lacked sufficient fruits and vegetables.

We were unable to perform surgeries, but we have been offered the use of a hospital in town if in the future we can bring a surgeon with us. Until then, we refer serious cases to doctors in Guatemala City. Sometimes we provide more than medical help. Rural pastor Noé González—age fifty-one, his white shirt emphasizing his dark hair and complexion as he entered our clinic—complained of chest and stomach pain. He had walked for two and a half hours to reach us. The advanced testing and X-rays that he would need in Huehuetenango

would cost four hundred quetzales (about $40), well beyond his means. We gave him the money.

A mother brought in a three-month-old baby that looked about six weeks old. Despite the day's seventy degrees, the little one wore a woolen hat, a sweater set, a sleeper, an undershirt, socks, a jacket, and two blankets. She was not eating well or thriving and only sucked half-heartedly at a bottle of some sort of rice water. The scrawny little body showed blotched, mottled skin, and a bad case of cradle cap on her head and thrush in her mouth.

First, explained the doctor with little hope (knowing how hard it is to convince people that widespread and long-standing customs are often wrong), the baby was much too hot. He removed the excess clothing, so carefully put on by the well-meaning mother, and left the child more comfortable. Second, the baby needed regular bathing. He patiently went through the procedure. Third, rice water did not hold the nutrition necessary for health and growth; the baby would need formula. He prescribed vitamins as well. Urging the mother to bring the baby back in a month, he turned to us as she left and whispered, "I don't think she's going to make it." Nevertheless, to our joy, he e-mailed us a few weeks later to report that the mother, having heeded his recommendations, had brought in the baby 100 percent improved.

Conditions are appalling, I will admit. As in much of Latin America, local sewers cannot take toilet paper, which is instead thrown into open wastebaskets. I just don't let it bother me. If you are fastidious about cleanliness, don't go. If you live to be punctual and can't put up with seven o'clock turning into eight-thirty, don't go. If you thrive on organization and can't roll with the punches and make do with substandard, substitute, or nonexistent equipment, don't go. If you absolutely need a shower every day and can't imagine cold or no water, or using a cup to gather enough drops to rinse your hair, don't go.

Why do I go? It's something I've always wanted to do. The joy I find in accomplishing something good lies beyond expression. I want to spend more time helping those who don't have what I do as I become ever more thankful for my many riches. These people don't speak English, yet they are warm, welcoming, and incredibly grateful. When I am there, I feel tempted not to return home. The country is beautiful; the people are colorful. They are also dirt poor, yet they don't feel sorry for themselves. This has made me see how much you can do without, as well as how much you can accomplish with little.

I can't say enough about my eagerness to go again. I want to make this an annual venture, and, in the future, when my family is more independent, to stay longer. These trips are probably the best thing I've ever done in my life. They sure beat lying out on the beach.

India

Volunteers in Medical Missions

Exhausted, Appreciated, Inspired

"People in the United States are spoiled.
You give, and they just want more.
In poverty-stricken countries like India,
the people really appreciate your help."

MURTICE SHEREK

REGISTERED NURSE AND CLINICAL ANALYST

The "Nurses Needed" advertisement in the medical paper announced an upcoming trip with Volunteers in Medical Missions, an interdenominational Christian organization that takes family practice medical help to developing countries. I had always felt the need to participate in something like this. My children were grown; my husband was trained; I had the money. Nothing was holding me back.

Since that trip to India, I have traveled on many missions with VIMM. By merit of being the first, that one remains most vivid in my mind. For most volunteers, their first trip proves the shocker, the eye opener into conditions in other parts of the world, the trip where they wonder what they have gotten themselves into. After a time, they become less stirred and saddened as repeated exposure inures them to the deplorable conditions in which much of humanity lives. That first trip, I knew nothing. Seeing so much on subsequent trips has left me less impressionable, more hardened, but no less determined to do what I can to help.

Poverty is poverty, whether it resides in Vietnam, Ukraine, Venezuela, Zimbabwe, or India, all countries to which I have traveled with VIMM. That said, India stands out in my mind, not as the country of my first mission, but as the country most overloaded with people and the one where I worked with leprosy.

We reached the Schieffelin Research and Training Centre by flying into Madras in southern India, then driving three hours to Karigiri. Leprosy didn't frighten me, but the driving did. Horns blared constantly, particularly at blind intersections where, without slowing, everyone tooted and barreled through. The bus we rode appeared to play chicken with all the other buses between Madras and the clinic; one or the other would veer off at the last possible minute. All on board applauded each time we didn't hit a bus. We actually did hit a scooter car, but bus and car continued on as though nothing had happened. Accidents and fender benders form part of the normal course of events in India.

The guest quarters at the Schieffelin resembled a barracks. Each held a toilet, a shower, and a sink hooked to a tube that went to a trough outside the building. The staff proved kind and helpful, providing us each day with a lunch of sandwiches, fruit, little bananas, and bottled water or soda. Since many of us had brought snacks from home, we often ended up giving our sack lunches to one of the immensely grateful poor people waiting to be seen. The staff also took good care of those team members who became ill—not from the food or the heat, but from an unknown airplane passenger who coughed the whole flight and left several of us infected with an upper respiratory bug.

I found the poverty incredible, the beggars heartbreaking. Women tried to give us their babies. Those with aspirations and abilities tried to go to school in India where they could afford tuition, but they aimed at reaching the United States to have a better life. We thought at times we recognized the oppressive caste system, but we did not consider ourselves sufficiently well versed in the culture to be certain or to ask. We did note that local doctors treated people kindly, unlike in Vietnam or Africa, where they could be downright rude.

Cows wandered everywhere, even in the city, enjoying a protected status under Hinduism. They did not compare, of course, to the big, fat cows we see in the States, but believers worshiped their skin-and-bone bodies anyway. On the facades of old buildings, goats—hungrier even than their owners—would lick a wall that had once held a poster.

I suppose they enjoyed some form of nutrition from the remaining glue. They ate any posters, as well.

The general population had no indoor toilets. On one of our drives, we passed five boys by the side of the road taking a communal poop. In the cities, sewage flowed in an open trough over which one had to step at the side of the street. The smell was horrible.

Mini businesses, ramshackle structures constructed from any available material, appeared one next to another. Women—dressed in colorful saris over a halter top with beads—carried heavy bundles on their heads and produced bricks or bamboo chairs in mini factories. Vendors sold from carts. Amid the tooting of car horns, oxen drew carts through narrow streets as vendors offered their wares and beggars extended their hands. Occasionally what looked like a flower-decorated float—the Indian equivalent of a hearse—passed amid music and firecrackers. The deceased man propped up in the middle stared unseeing at the crowd as he rode, we assumed, to his cremation.

Rural villages that drew schoolchildren from the countryside consisted typically of a school, a grocery, a couple other businesses, a large temple, and clay-walled houses with roofs of straw or corrugated tin. Each little home had openings for a door and windows without actually having any. One offered a single chair as the total furnishing. Women cooked over open fires. This, along with the general dirtiness, explained many of the cases of burning eyes and chest congestion we treated. Yet these humble one-room homes included a cow shelter, often better than the houses themselves.

Medically as well as geographically, India lies a world away. As we passed the huge hospital in Velore, we saw used and washed dressings hanging out to dry. Nurses wore white saris over a white halter top as a uniform. The Indian pharmacists were brilliant, yet their knowledge proved of limited use, as they had little to work with.

The Schieffelin staff, though extensively experienced in lower limb prosthetics, had seen little arm loss. A missionary who was traveling with us demonstrated to these intrigued doctors and therapists the wide range of functions she could carry out with her two arm prostheses. For the fingerless and otherwise deformed patients at the leprosy center, however, such possibilities remained beyond imagination, both financially and culturally. Indian norms dictate that food—no matter how sloppy—be eaten with the fingers rather than with utensils. Mechanical devices cannot replace human digits in this culture.

I wasn't worried about the leprosy. Rather, I found myself interested, even fascinated. I had read what I could to prepare. I was not prepared, however, for the stigma associated with leprosy in India. In the United States, while the disease is rare, we have the possibility of enlightening our more educated population to the fact that leprosy is a low-contagion disease that is not only treatable, but curable if caught in time. In India, on the other hand, prominent citizens and once highly regarded businessmen, when diagnosed with leprosy, can come to nothing in the space of a few months, cast out by their own society.

The doctors, like all our Indian coworkers, were proud, intelligent, and well trained. By screening for leprosy, they complemented our regular family practice offerings. We traveled out each day to rural clinics organized by the local Rotary Club, offering a total of twelve doctors. The Indian doctors did indeed discover several new leprosy cases that we would have attributed to more mundane skin disorders. We, of course, see leprosy only in textbooks; they see it in the flesh.

Along with ten others, I staffed the pharmacy. The first three days proved difficult, as seventeen of our medicine crates and suitcases failed to arrive with us. British Airways only flew into Madras once every three days, so we had no choice but to offer the first clinics with limited stock plus some purchased Indian medicines. We expanded our selection when the lost pieces arrived.

We spread our medicines on a single table around which eight of us counted pills and filled one prescription after another. Three others dispensed the medicines to an Indian pharmacist who educated the patients on their use. A native pharmacist translated the prescriptions written in Sanskrit. Along with each medicine we gave a gift of soap, a toothbrush, toothpaste, or other small and needed item. The temperature floated in the nineties. The humidity and the bustle of eleven people in a single room made it hotter. Outside, a mass of humanity unacquainted with the custom of waiting in line pushed and shoved to get to the front.

Each day we saw hundreds, literally. An American doctor stopped his work one day to tell us we had to move faster. We told him politely but firmly that he should go back and take care of patients, and we would take care of the pharmacy. He later apologized. Until you've worked it yourself, you have no idea how hard pharmacy work is under these conditions. Doing the best we could, we made it through each day, then dropped exhausted at night.

Ceremony forms an integral part of Indian culture. After each clinic, the local Rotary Club formally thanked us for our help, giving us long necklaces, wicker baskets, metal peacocks, and other remembrances, along with protracted speeches of gratitude. The uneducated population proved grateful as well. People in the United States are spoiled. You give, and they just want more. In poverty-stricken countries, like India, the people really appreciate your help.

I need to do this work. I have a skill to share, and I miss it if I don't. I also realize that I'm very wealthy and very lucky. I have to help those who have so much less, even if only with a smile. As exhausted as I may feel while I'm there, I don't return that way. I come back inspired.

Honduras

International Health Service

Where the Rivers Are Highways

*"To get any mail to them, you have to get it to the pilot in La Ceiba,
who flies it to the minister in Puerto Lempira,
who will hand deliver it the next time he canoes out their way."*

HAROLD PANUSKA
RETIRED SURGEON

I first traveled to Honduras in 1970, enthused by the insistence of a friend with previous experience in that country. Solo practice limited my out-of-office time, so a two-week mission with the Christian Medical Society fit my situation. I continued with this group for ten years.

In the course of these missions I heard about La Mosquitia, that isolated, sparsely populated lowland expanse in the eastern part of the country, bordered by Nicaragua and the Caribbean, transversed by rivers and pounded by seasonal rains. There was little if any medical help there, I was told, and this attracted me.

The Christian Medical Society refused to let us go there because of the lack of evangelical churches to host us. This refusal only fueled the discontent already felt by various members regarding CMS's strict rules, so, in 1980, the man who had first invited me to Honduras and I formed International Health Service as a secular, nondenominational alternative. Our first team consisted of fifteen volunteers. The organization now claims over one hundred. We include no preaching on our missions, only medical attention.

Forming a nonprofit organization was no easy task. We had to file interminable paperwork, write bylaws and a constitution, and demonstrate our eligibility for tax exemption. We plugged away, not letting the red tape deter us. Our goal—to become a registered and reputable group—would lead not only to tax exemption, but to a listing with the State Department as an organization recognized for doing our type of work. This, in turn, would lead to more volunteers and to legitimization with the Honduran government. Involving Hondurans in our projects formed one of the organization's major objectives.

We had originally envisioned IHS working in a different country every year. That never happened for two reasons. First, the logistics of getting organized in Honduras—forming contacts with the Minister of Health, the Minister of Housing, and other Honduran organizations—proved so time consuming that the prospect of trying to repeat this process every year in a different country appeared overly daunting. Second, the need in Honduras proved so overwhelming that we felt no choice but to return year after year.

From those early years, Carl Platou, then hospital administrator of Fairview, backed us with donations of medical supplies, extension cords, generators, dental chairs, and other equipment. This unnamed system of donations eventually became organized into the Fairview Foundation Medical Missions program, which continues to sponsor employees who are willing to donate their time and talents to the less fortunate of the world.

At the beginning, we would catch a single weekly flight from the major port of La Ceiba to the more remote Puerto Lempira in La

Mosquitia. Once there, we either drove an old truck over the one existing road or paddled canoes up the rivers, where we would stay in a village for two or three days, then paddle on to the next.

That first year, we arrived largely unexpected. In Puerto Lempira, we had to spend an entire day parleying and explaining our mission to the local authorities before being allowed to work. In years since, the Honduran government has flown us in on a vintage DC3. At present, we work with Wings of Hope, which supplies us with planes and pilots to service the small grass runways in remote villages.

Flying into La Mosquitia in those early years, we entered another world. The people spoke not Spanish, but Mosquito. Naked children swam out to meet our canoe as we neared remote villages. Men followed age-old slash-and-burn techniques to plant their corn, sharing their harvest with the entire village. One man would own a pig, another a cow. When anyone butchered, the entire village ate. The same held true of the rice harvest or fish caught from the river. People bartered with pigs, chickens, fish, rice, and corn.

This twentieth century culture still existed without the wheel. I never saw a wheelbarrow or a wagon. Heavy loads were dragged on the ground behind a donkey; moderate loads were carried by women on their heads. Women performed most of the work, eternally gathering and carrying firewood for their cooking or scrubbing laundry on the rocks in the river. Villagers—lacking a well—used a coconut shell to dip river water out of a big pit as it filtered through the sand. There were no sanitation facilities.

Some of this has changed with time and assistance from the Peace Corps and other groups. Primitive schools—thatched huts with open sides—offer instruction by a villager or minister of limited training. Clothing can be bought in Puerto Lempira or received from various donating organizations. Before, the people made their garments,

sharing one foot-treadled sewing machine among six or seven villages.

Some things remain unchanged. In this remote area, where water continues to be the only mode of transportation, men still build *cayucas,* or canoes, carved from a large tree. These range from one-person *cayucas* to those that fit five or six people plus their gear. Having no electricity or machinery, the men cut through giant mahogany logs set upon stilts. Using a two-person saw, one man above and another below, they drive wedges into the log to keep the saw from binding.

As we moved from village to village, people who failed to receive medical attention in their own village simply followed us downriver in their *cayucas* to the next. At one of these river villages, little Nori—six years old and with the dark hair, round face, and Honduran features common to the area— was brought in by her father to have her teeth examined. She had been blind from birth. Sitting in our portable dental chair in the darkened hut, she twisted her head toward the only window. I moved the chair to get a better view, and again she turned her head toward the light. I called in another doctor. After examination, we came to the conclusion that she had some retinal activity. We arranged to have her brought back to the States, where eye surgeons operated and gave her the gift of sight. Nori had never before seen her mother. When we returned her to Honduras, the reunion turned into a session of joyous tears, as mother and daughter hugged and cried together. The overjoyed mother gave me what she had—two eggs—to say thank you for her daughter's sight.

Because she could see, Nori was able to attend school and learn to read. She must be twenty-five or twenty-six by now. I still hear from her and her father now and again. Mail, of course, remains difficult. To send me a letter, they have to take it by canoe to Puerto Lempira and get it to the occasional pilot to mail in La Ceiba. In reverse, to get any mail to them, I have to get it to the pilot in La Ceiba, who flies it to the minister in Puerto Lempira, who will hand deliver it the next time he canoes out their way.

Teenage José had lost three of his limbs in a banana train accident. We brought him to Minnesota, where Fairview doctors attached prosthetic legs and an arm. Today, back in Honduras, José is raising a family, supporting them by selling pop and cigarettes from a little stand.

Not all cases prove so dramatic. We see a lot of machete injuries, do a lot of extractions, remove a lot of tumors. Perhaps "nondramatic" is a poor qualifier. I have taken out a carcinoma as big as a golf ball from a man's mouth. Helped by generators, suction machines, and local anesthesia, we have rebroken and reset fractures that had self-healed at a ninety-degree angle. We have given antibiotics and marveled at their rapid effect on people never before exposed to them. We have removed masses of worms so large they obstructed people's bowels. While we automatically deworm patients, we recognize that as long as they walk barefoot among the excrement from their animals, they will continue to be reinfected.

You never know what to expect. I was awakened once in the middle of the night to attend a man injured in a machete fight. Blood spurted from the severed artery in his right arm. With nothing but local anesthesia, we managed to tie it off and keep him alive overnight until a plane (notified by my ham radio) could get him to the hospital we had helped build in Puerto Lempira. He survived. At an earlier time, he would have died during the four- or five-day canoe trip, and there would have been no hospital at the end of the waterway, even if he had survived that long.

It's hard to explain to people how exciting this work is. I have taken my three boys with me as helpers, and all three have found it a tremendous experience. You have to be fit. It's rustic; you eat reconstituted food and sleep in sleeping bags under mosquito netting on the floors of churches or schools. Most people do very well. I go every year—sometimes twice—and stay five weeks at a time. I set my own schedule, working from six to six, undisturbed by artificialities such as daylight-saving time, undistracted by modern practices such as sending out invoices. I just work. When I leave and realize what I've accomplished, it makes a new person out of me. I feel good.

Russia, Vietnam

Resource Exchange International

Former Enemies, Future Friends

"They think Americans can do anything."

JOHN HUFF
RETIRED OTOLARYNGOLOGIST

My wife and I had already planned our long-awaited vacation to Alaska when I learned from fellow physicians that a local church sending a team to Russia needed an ear, nose, and throat specialist. I hesitated. The team was to leave only a week after our return from Alaska. Furthermore, many of the group followed more fundamentalist doctrines than I, a strait-laced Norwegian Lutheran. Nevertheless, my wife and I agreed that this offered a wonderful opportunity, one I shouldn't pass up.

I did not consider myself unacquainted with conditions in developing countries. As an Air Force flight surgeon stationed in Germany, I had worked in northern Africa. The 1995 trip to Russia, however, was my first experience with a civilian mission. While the church group that organized it no longer exists, my experience proved so positive that I followed it with a trip to Vietnam under the auspices of Resource Exchange International.

REI can use people in agriculture, medicine, and other lines of work to teach and share equipment and technologies. In-country representatives inform locals of the upcoming visit and line up an itinerary. In our case, we accompanied local doctors as they saw their patients.

Some organizations (no criticism intended) take American doctors to do surgeries normally unavailable to local people; local doctors learn only by watching. REI's philosophy, however, dictates that we teach the people to do for themselves. When a local doctor preparing to operate politely deferred to me and offered me the drill, I smiled and said, "No, you do it." We ended up performing the operation as a joint effort.

In both Russia and Vietnam, I found local physicians capable but hampered by a pathetic lack of equipment. In the city of Hue, I discovered a doctor who performed mastoidectomies (the opening of the bone behind the ear to drain pus) with gouges and chisels, as he had no mastoid drill. He did a beautiful job. I saw another resourceful doctor performing mastoidectomies with a decrepit dental drill. A middle-aged physician listened to my interpreted discussion of drill work with longing. He finally asked whether he could have my mastoid drill when I left. Unfortunately, I felt obligated to leave it in the larger city of Hanoi, where a greater number of doctors would make use of it.

Despite the lack of equipment, we teach. Our urologist taught new procedures possible with the equipment available. Another doctor brought heart valves and taught the accompanying procedures, which would be useful as long as the supply of valves lasted. Nevertheless, lack of equipment proved to be only one of the problems affecting doctors in Russia and Vietnam.

Vietnam produces too many doctors who only want to live in cities. Politics largely determines who can become a doctor in a large city. If you have a doctor for a father, or if you are related to someone important, you might have a chance. For the rest, the only careers lie in small villages where no one wants to go. If urban Vietnam is Third World, the rural areas rate a Fourth World classification, medical equipment being nonexistent. So it is that three-fourths of each graduating medical class ends up driving cabs or performing other work below their educational level. They find no place in the medical world.

In Russia, I lived with a doctor's family. He earned about $100 a month. Family members made ends meet by hunting, fishing, and picking berries. Ex-communist countries don't pay doctors more than other workers, yet these underpaid, overworked physicians care for their patients as much as any doctor here.

I worked in the hospital in Russia for some time, getting to know the doctors on a personal basis. One of them, suffering from a lingering infection, needed to have his eardrum patched, which I did with local anesthesia. He embraced us all as bosom friends, taking us along with fellow Russians on huge picnics in the forest. I reflected on how during the Cold War we believed that Russians were so terrible. Perhaps because they have had so little contact with the outside world, they welcomed us with open arms. Were the situation reversed, I wondered, would we treat them as well?

In Vietnam, where students formerly studied Russian, they now learn English. This gorgeous country is home to warm, wonderful people. It is a mind-opening experience to meet your ex-enemy.

The people of both countries hold Americans in high esteem. My examination of a Russian woman showed that her ear canals had never developed. Correction for this problem involves difficult, technical surgery that we couldn't possibly teach in the time we had or perform with available equipment. This inability proved a big disappointment, since Russians think Americans can do anything.

Having traveled to foreign countries, I can affirm that it is not as difficult or frightening as many Americans think. You go to be nice, to represent America, to share. The opportunity benefits both sides. It boils down to people being the same the world over and wonderful year round.

I remember the hobos that occasionally came around during my childhood in the early 1930s. My mother always gave them food and let them sleep in the barn. That's how we used to be in this country. With time and a surfeit of information on countrywide crimes and atrocities, we have lost that openness. We've become more suspicious, insular, and self-protective. If you read the news too much, you become afraid to do anything. The people of developing countries remain more open and welcoming to strangers.

"What could I do?" is the question I hear most from fence-sitters who want to go on a mission but don't quite dare. They have no clue how useful their abilities are in a developing country. They are mistaken if they think they have no skills. Most people in poor countries will never have the possibility of travel. For them, the very fact that we visit becomes a gift. Many are thrilled just to practice their English with a native speaker.

In May, I will complete three years of retirement. I keep up with eight children and fourteen grandchildren, maintain the house and yard, and drive a hearse and limousine, but I want to go back. When I do, I want to take some young people with me. They need to be initiated into this fantastic experience.

El Salvador

Great Commission to Latin America

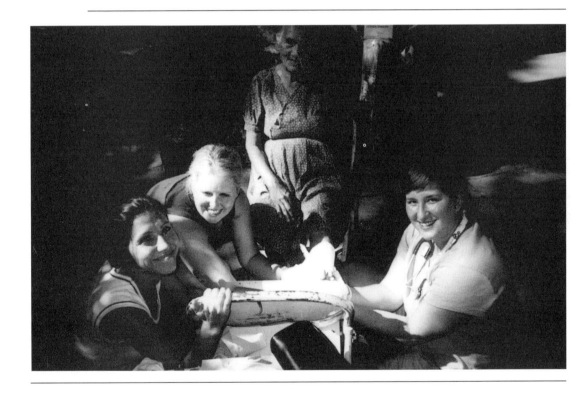

Building a New Jerusalem

*"In order that all might have a new home, families moved in together—
extended families of aunts, uncles, and grandparents,
plus numerous children."*

GENEVIEVE HOLMEN

REGISTERED NURSE

The Great Commission to Latin America claims as members many interdenominational Christian churches in the United States, Europe, and Latin America itself. The organization's core philosophy revolves around ministering to underdeveloped countries. Although I am only twenty-two, I have always felt called to this type of work. Information from a pastor at my parents' church led me to this particular organization, and I took off for El Salvador, with brand-new nursing license in hand. I didn't know another soul on the team except for the pastor.

I had been to Mexico as a tourist, but I went unprepared for the throngs of people that surrounded us from the moment the plane touched ground in the capital city, San Salvador. These needy people believed that we, being American and white, would be able to help.

We lived dormitory style in a mission house—complete with indoor plumbing and electricity—of the Great Commission in San Salvador. Bug spray limited our contact with some of the unwanted insects. As we slept on mats on the floor, however, we never could isolate ourselves completely from the roaches. Talk about big! Apart from the unavoidable creepy crawlies, however, the place was clean. The cook, trained in preparing food for gringos, made us lunches of hot dogs, peanut butter and jelly, or tuna sandwiches.

Like many mission groups, we tackled both medical and construction problems. Eight of us formed the medical team; the other sixteen went to build housing for those left homeless by recent earthquakes. Each day we traveled two hours out of San Salvador to the town of Jerusalén (Jerusalem, as we would say). The earthquake had leveled 90 percent of the structures there, leaving many of the two thousand inhabitants homeless. The construction team worked with Samaritan's Purse, which funded the materials, and with the families who would receive the houses, who provided additional labor. Team members brought their own tools. The houses they built measured perhaps twenty by twenty-four feet and had two rooms—a kitchen/living area and a bedroom. A foundation of two-thirds soil and one-third concrete supported cement blocks held together with mortar. These, in turn, held up a corrugated tin roof. There was no indoor plumbing, no gas or electricity, no doors and windows—only openings in the walls. Yet, desperate as they were, in order that all might have a new home, families moved in together—extended families of aunts, uncles, and grandparents, plus numerous children.

Americans may wonder how anyone could be eager for a home that might cool down to seventy at night but heats up under a tin roof to ninety or a hundred during the day, a home without the cooking or bathroom facilities that we take for granted. The truth is, the people of Jerusalén have never known these luxuries and don't miss them. As in many crowded countries, they spend little time in the home during the day. They consider it a place to take meals and sleep and find protection from the elements, nothing more.

While the construction group labored in the sun, we set up a clinic under a huge tree in the Jerusalén town square. Too few buildings remained standing to offer an indoor clinic. We stepped carefully over uneven ground, as the concrete of the plaza had buckled and folded during the tremors. As for the pharmacy, we did the best we could, arranging our medicines around the massive trunk of a tree, which had somehow survived the ravages the buildings had not. On the first two days, we handed out numbers to the crowd. On the third day, realizing we couldn't see everyone, we triaged.

The majority suffered from skin and intestinal infections due to the poor sanitation. Without treatment, rashes and cuts become infected easily, especially in the tropical heat. For these ailments, we had medicines. We suffered, however, from a lack of casting supplies, at least on the first day. Because it was already several months after the earthquake, we had assumed that other groups would have visited before us, splinting legs and taking care of fractures. Not so. Numerous patients came to us with their bones broken and unset after all these months. Happily, we found a closet of supplies in the mission house, and on the second day we treated not only new patients but also the ones we had patched together with pieces of wood and newspaper the day before.

One of these was Santos. About five feet tall with the dark skin and stoic, well-defined features of her Indian ancestry, she hobbled over in a worn, cotton blue-print dress. Her coming was announced by the slap-slap of her turquoise thongs, "my only shoes," she said. At seventy-four years, she was walking on a broken tibia and fibula and

had been doing so for the several months since the earthquake. She suffered terrible pain, as the bones separated with every movement, but she was the wife of a farmer, and what choice did she have? We gave her Tylenol while we set the bone and prepared to put on a cast. Her sudden agitation registered more than the discomfort of the bone setting. Through the interpreter, we understood that she wanted no part of a cast if it meant that she couldn't wear her "shoes." So we made the cast in such a way that her toes stuck out enough to fit into her turquoise thongs.

"I think I'm going to have to convert to Christianity," she declared via the interpreter, shocking us with this sudden burst of candor. "The priests and nuns have never come to help us." Like most of the inhabitants of Jerusalén, she had been a lifelong Catholic. Why she thought that her faith was something other than Christianity, I cannot guess.

As to why her own church had not offered help, I can only assume that either the great prevalence of poverty has left it inured to the sufferings of its members, or, more likely, the help it is able to offer cannot possibly cover the vast need. To give an example, the average Salvadoran makes about 1,000 colones a month. A simple tube of antibacterial ointment costs 120.

We spent three days in Jerusalén, seven in La Libertad. Whereas Jerusalén stands in the mountains and can access a fresh water supply, La Libertad lies on the hot coastal plain and cannot. Public water is available via hand pump at a central well, where people line up from the beginning of the day. No sewage system exists, and somewhere along the line the sewage and water mix, as demonstrated by the undue number of intestinal problems.

In the humid, one-hundred-degree or higher heat, we held our clinic in a church. This turned out to be hotter than the outdoors. For bathroom facilities, we shared a single outhouse with the patients.

A mother, desperate but stoic, carried in a four-year-old with a temperature of 106 degrees. The little girl had been unable to eat or drink for several days and was badly dehydrated. She weighed only twenty-five pounds. The bright red of her cotton dress stood in stark contrast to her mental and physical stupor, as she proved nearly impossible to awaken. Without treatment, she had perhaps another twenty-four hours to live. We gave her a broad-spectrum antibiotic for her intestinal infection and IV fluids. As she became able, we offered her sips of water mixed with salt, sugar, and potassium.

This little one made it, hanging out with us for the next couple of days. Her eager showing-off of a few English words and phrases provided a complete contrast to her earlier state of semiawareness. Her mother confided that she had lost two children in the last two years from similar infections. She still had eight other children, three younger and five older. Like most women of her class, she had no birth control available other than the rhythm method.

The Bible tells us that "the poor you will always have with you." Certainly in my lifetime, the problem of poverty cannot be solved. Nevertheless, I drastically changed several people's lives and saved a few others. In ten days, our team members built forty houses.

A short-term mission gives you a new perspective on life. It extends your ability to appreciate what you have and to realize what you can live without. Happiness is a state of mind, not of belongings. Someday, when my college debt is repaid, I want to do mission work on a permanent basis. I will move to Latin America and work for the Great Commission. Should I meet someone, he will have to share the same values. Either we'll both stay, or we'll go on a continual series of return missions.

Tanzania

Lutheran Order of Discipleship

Where the Churches Are Full

"We saw lots of young and old people,
but few between ages twenty-five and forty-five.
They're dead of AIDS.
Large portions of the population are just gone."

JOEL WIBERG
PASTOR

As a young pastor, I spent five and a half years as a missionary in Africa. For thirty years, I have retained both the Swahili I learned and the affection I developed for the people of Tanzania. In 1998, I returned under the auspices of the Lutheran Order of Discipleship.

Until my recent retirement, I worked as a psychotherapist at the Fairview Counseling Centers. In the United States, we have various counseling options, many covered in part via health insurance or offered free at county mental health centers. In Tanzania, not only are mental health personnel few and far between, but there is no insurance coverage for the poor. For these reasons, the role of pastoral counselor takes on even greater importance in the African communities than here in the United States. So it was that I spent four weeks in Tanzania helping pastors-in-training with their counseling skills.

Two hours from the town of Bukoba on the western shore of Lake Victoria, one finds the Lutheran Theological College, part of a boarding seminary supported by the diocese. The students here have gained a secondary education or secondary plus two years. After three additional years of theology, they find themselves relatively well educated compared to the rest of the population.

A breakdown in the educational system during the last three decades has left teachers poorly paid. As a result, not as many good people enter the profession, and teachers have lost much of the respect they once had. The clergy, on the other hand, remains highly regarded. African cultures, spiritually oriented to the core, look to religious leaders, making their role as counselors all the more important.

The church forms the center of culture in many places, creating a significant force in African society. It often constitutes the only organizing force in rural areas and remains a major factor even in urban settings. At a typical service, the women come dressed in colorful *kitengas,* their babies wrapped on their backs. The men appear well dressed in suits and ties. The service offers a liturgy similar to a Lutheran service or Catholic mass in the States. The sermon, on the other hand, lasts notably longer than those to which we are accustomed. No organ or piano music accompanies the service. The people sing a cappella, swaying and clapping to the rhythm. They love music and know the hymns well. At one time, most of the hymns came from Europe. Many still do, but more and more, hymns are emerging out of the African musical heritage.

I found the churches notably full, the high attendance spurred in part by the fear of AIDS. A large proportion of the people in every congregation has been affected in one way or another by this dreaded disease. We saw lots of young and old people, but few between ages twenty-five and forty-five. They're dead of AIDS. Large portions of the population are just gone.

While no exact figures are available, it is estimated that 25 to 40 percent of the people of Bukoba would test HIV-positive. Of the city's twenty-five thousand people, that would mean roughly six to ten thousand. A well-known pastor in his sixties, typical of many, has lost four sons to AIDS, leaving him and his wife to care for the grandchildren. This loss, in African culture, implies even more than it does here, as the passing on of a name takes on greater importance to them than to us. To lose one's male heirs is to lose one's lineage, to fail to perpetuate one's family line. This traumatic loss repeats itself over and over in African society today.

So what counseling does a pastor offer in Tanzania? To a great degree, the same as here: marriage and family, alcohol abuse, some drug abuse. AIDS counseling plays a bigger role. So many are either dying of the disease themselves or related to someone who is. Pastoral counselors stress clean and responsible living to avoid getting or spreading the disease. They also spend a lot of time listening to the fears and concerns of those who already have it, to the families who are about to lose a loved one, to the grandparents caring for the grandchildren, and to the parentless children, many already condemned to die far short of their normal life span.

The Lutheran Order of Discipleship no longer exists, but the Christian-based counseling skills I taught remain. Whether in the United States or in Tanzania, in the face of AIDS and other afflictions, pastoral care and counseling offer solace and hope.

Haiti

Friendship Church, Hands of Friendship

For Just One Better Day

"You learn to appreciate a smile, because the people have nothing else."

RHAE ANN GRINDELAND

EMERGENCY MEDICAL TECHNICIAN

What began as an evangelical mission in Haiti expanded to encompass other areas as the need for food, medicine, and clothing became apparent. Hands of Friendship, a mission team from Friendship Church in Prior Lake, Minnesota, raises money through its thrift shop. Some of the items donated go directly to Haiti in truckloads. The others, sold to the public, generate money, which supports the mission in a remote region of this poverty-stricken country.

I had just made a career change from accounting to medicine when I read a note in my church bulletin one Sunday. "Medical supplies needed," it said. Most of what they were asking for consisted of over-the-counter medicines, things I could obtain easily through my work at the hospital. I could do this and consider it part of my tithe.

I phoned the woman in charge of the team to ascertain the needs. In the course of our conversation, I managed to blurt out, "I wish I could do what you're doing someday." After a moment of silence, she asked, "Why not go with us this time?" I never anticipated how that conversation would impact my life.

I had not traveled out of the country before, and I doubted and ruminated as the idea slowly consumed me. In the end, I gathered medical supplies, got the vital documents, and took the necessary precautions—shots for hepatitis A and B and pills for malaria. I left afraid but excited, the final words of the nurse from the travel clinic still fresh in my ears: "There's a lot of AIDS down there. Be careful!"

That trip led to three others, the latest in 1997. That year, recently divorced and a single mom, I was no longer able to comfortably pay the trip to Haiti. Yet I felt I needed to go. I sent in my application for a Fairview grant, but heard nothing. Denied, I thought. October came, and so did the time to turn in the money. I used what I had carefully saved for car insurance, believing that somehow, I would be able to replace it. Three days before Christmas, I received the grant from Fairview, enabling me to pay my car insurance. God provides if he really wants you there and if you trust him.

At the airport, United Nations troops had surrounded our plane the moment it landed. Armed soldiers stood at the gates of the airport to quell any unrest. There seemed good excuse for unrest: an ever-widening dichotomy between rich and poor and a corrupt government that did nothing to alleviate the situation. Sometimes it made it worse. As we passed through customs with our bags of medicines and clothing, the agents took what they wanted for themselves. We were powerless to do anything about it.

Haiti ranks among the poorest nations in our hemisphere. Scores of people thronged at the airport begging "Dollah! Dollah!," their hands outstretched in the hope that they might receive something. One woman, desiring a better life for her child, handed her baby over to our team leader, catching her totally off guard. "Wait!"

called the astonished woman as she ran after the mother. "I can't keep this baby!"

The country, although not at war, appeared war torn. Buildings crumbled. The streets looked bombed. Everything stood in need of maintenance and repair. People surged all about. Horns honked; men hung off the sides and backs of trucks, making use of overcrowded transportation. Amid this massive swell of humanity, we stood out as minority white people. Hundreds of black faces stared at us, and we stared back in shock and awe at what we were seeing.

Our team traveled atop duffel bags in the bed of a large truck through parts of Port-au-Prince, where the sickening stench of human waste rose into the air. Garbage lay strewn everywhere, as children grew up with the adults' example of throwing everything on the ground.

With time, I figured out a temporary solution for the garbage. I had candy. The kids wanted it. I wanted the garbage picked up. By pantomime, I let them know the game. Soon I had bags and bags of garbage, and the children had their candy. While this provides an amusing anecdote, the fact remains that living in filth breeds sickness and disease. As a result, part of our program concentrated on teaching basic hygiene. Despite the filthy environment, we found the people themselves remarkably clean, with the exception of those working in construction. No one smelled, and we didn't see any lice.

Our truck suffered breakdowns the entire way. My food—jostled, sat on, and wet from the rain—metamorphosed into a crumbled mess. Ten hours out of Port-au-Prince, we neared our destination, a village nestled on a mountainside. When the truck refused to go further, we had no alternative but to unload the crates, bags, and ourselves and head up the mountain on foot. As we began, Haitian people appeared out of nowhere, heaving our crates onto their own backs or their donkeys'. They carried everything for us but our water bottles. Everything arrived intact.

That night, many of the good people gave up their tin-roofed homes for us. We rested, considering the work before us. Our team, consisting of carpenters, teachers, and a medical contingent, planned to finish the village's partially constructed, badly needed clinic. The long-range goal focused on getting it up and running and then training Haitians to take it over.

Everywhere we went, people dressed in donated clothing (I chuckled at Vikings T-shirts in Haiti), making the typical attire a faded reflection of our own. In this varied apparel, people came to worship in churches with holes for windows, cement floors, and trees shaved to make flat benches. The services, in Creole, lasted up to two and a half hours. People sang, praised, and threw their hands in the air as their whole bodies entered the rhythm of a fast and upbeat form of worship that manifested their African heritage.

Work at the clinic was difficult. Over time, some of the items and equipment left by previous teams had disappeared. Stolen by the government? By locals? There was no telling. Bad apples could be found anywhere, we told ourselves. Nevertheless, it proved discouraging. How could we help the Haitians to help themselves, how could we teach them to become self-sufficient, if a few among them were defeating this purpose?

I was further discouraged after speaking with two Haitian doctors, whom I met toward the end of one of my trips. They were wonderful men who practiced in a Haitian community in the United States, generating funds to improve conditions in their country. We showed them some of the videotapes we had made of various Haitian clinics. Our interpreters, they told us, were not good. Various maladies had been misdiagnosed because of poor translation. This corroborated some of

what I had observed on previous occasions. A patient would point to his or her eye, and the nurse would write "eye problem." Or was the patient pointing to his or her head to indicate a headache? I had also heard, on occasion, of well-meaning nonmedical people dispensing incorrect doses of medications. By providing these medications, were we unknowingly doing more harm than good?

My saddest encounter had to do with an American nurse whose heart was not in her work. "It looks good on a resume," she told me when I asked her why she had come. Upset by her attitude, I walked down from the mountain to the ocean with a couple of Haitian nurses. Poor as the country is, it still offers Pepsi and Coke. We sat together on the beach, digging our toes into the sand and drinking our Cokes. A common career bound us together while our languages kept us apart. Not to be deterred, we began pointing to different parts of our bodies, each saying the word in her own language and practicing the other's word, laughing together in the joy of a shared connection.

We played together in the ocean, they in their skirts and blouses, I in my long denim dress and T-shirt. They showed me how to dig in the sand for shells, open them, and recognize the different animals inside. Some were good for heartburn, some for other things. I realized how important these natural resources become to people when they can't obtain fabricated medicines. I had as much to learn from them as they from me.

I continued to question the validity of what we were doing. Pushing patients through at assembly line speed bothered me, but what alternative was there? What if, through poor translation, a patient did not understand that he or she had to take *all* of the antibiotic we were providing? Taking a partial dose would only raise resistance to the bacteria we were trying to kill.

I believe in miracles, but I also believe that we have to help them happen. We needed more medical personnel. I saw the need to spread the word and encourage my coworkers to join the effort to give undoctored people the adequate medical care they deserved.

That proved to be my last trip with Hands of Friendship, but the organization continues to draw dedicated people focused on helping those in need. Among its many worthwhile accomplishments, its greatest, in my view, lies in making so many people aware of the Haitian people's need and the conditions in which they live.

I retain some unforgettable memories. One evening I went for a walk, rather foolishly, alone. My dress got caught on a stick along the path. Someone reached out from among the trees to free my skirt. I heard laughter, but never saw who it was. I experienced the same sensation I felt on my first trip, when numerous white eyes in dark faces peeked out at us from between shadowy trees.

"They shoot white people there," my father-in-law had warned me before I left. His words returned to me my first night in Haiti as another woman and I slept on the porch of the pastor's house, just three blocks from the home of the voodoo priest. At 2:00 A.M. I awoke to the sound of chanting and the sight of torches moving toward us from a distance. While our house itself stood barricaded behind high walls, we lay exposed on the porch, cut off from the rest of the house. The chanting grew louder; the torch lights drew closer. I shivered as I remembered my father-in-law's words. My friend and I huddled together singing "Jesus Loves Me" until the chanting ceased sometime before dawn.

Voodoo practitioners, the pastor explained when we related our experience, commonly use such tactics to try to scare people. They did a fair job of it, I reflected, knowing that only my faith had seen me through those fearful hours.

On another occasion, we rode in a truck that had a cross hanging in the front window. Suddenly a wild-looking woman with glassy eyes appeared out of nowhere and began a voodoo dance around the truck, her white dress striking a notable contrast with her skin and disheveled black hair.

We lay low, watching our Ps and Qs. It was election time, a period of unrest and killing. American newspapers and television never covered what really went on; I saw guns pointed at people's heads as they voted.

Political unrest proved more or less a constant, even when elections were not imminent. On one occasion we sat in a church service attended by President Aristide's cousin, who had some political position of import. We could sense a crowd gathering outside. As the service went on, we heard shattering glass and the repeated thuds of his car being stoned by angry countrymen. On another of our trips, this cousin was badly beaten. Yet, after the nocturnal fright caused by the voodoo chanters, I never felt unsafe myself.

I left on my first trip with the idea that I could change the world. Instead, it changed me. This work strengthened my self-worth as it enlarged my desire to do more. It fortified me as a human being. I'm in college now, studying to be a nurse. In the past, I had never felt smart enough. My first mission trip convinced me that I could, indeed, do this.

It convinced me also that I want to be a medical missionary. I saw how much an increased number of medical personnel could offer these people. The pathetic need of those with no healthcare remains ever in my thoughts.

Currently, I work full-time and take care of my two teenage children. I collect medical supplies that people in the States can't use or that are overstocked, as well as medical equipment such as thermometers. All this I funnel into missions one way or another.

For now, I help others to go. I am improving my skills for use on a medical mission in the future. I will consider my efforts successful if I can give the unfortunate people I have seen just one better day.

Anyone who goes to a different culture and lives a different life for two weeks comes back a different person. You become grateful for the small things. You learn to appreciate a smile, because the people have nothing else. Despite the language barrier, you make friends.

On my last night in Haiti, as I packed my bags to return home, several children peered into my room in hopes of receiving some of the items I planned to leave behind. Among them appeared a beautiful eight-year-old boy.

As much as I longed to hug my own children again, the thought of leaving this little one tugged at my heart. His determination and desire to learn marked him as someone who might one day prove instrumental in changing his country. He had been trying to teach me Creole while learning English himself. With his English book tucked under his arm, he had come for another lesson. The sight of my bags wiped the happiness from his face.

"You going home?" he queried in broken English.

"Yeah," I replied, my throat tightening, "I'm going home."

He started to cry.

Sudan

World Vision

Eating Grass and Boiling Cowhide

"When malnutrition is long and severe, when death becomes a constant companion, the drive for self-preservation supersedes even maternal instinct, and mothers will eat the food meant for the children."

KAREN EASTERDAY

REGISTERED NURSE

It's easy to get depressed.

In Sudan, average life expectancy runs some twenty years fewer than in the United States, even less in the famished south. Infant mortality rates climb to ten times those here. Years of civil war have pushed thousands of people from their land; years of drought have left once arable land barren.

At one time, there were cattle. The men of the village would follow their grazing in a seminomadic existence, getting milk and meat from them and using them as money. Every woman knew her bride price in cows. Now, with famine, war, and large migrations of dislocated people, the grass has become scarce and so have the cattle.

When an adult male with listless eyes and protruding ribs staggers into the feeding center and collapses, when a gaunt-faced mother wearing nothing but a wraparound skirt brings in a stick-limbed baby with barely the strength to suckle, I don't get emotionally involved or I won't get done what I have to do. I busy myself trying to get everybody fed, trying to boil water for milk, trying to keep people alive. I don't have time for depression. I'll deal with it afterward.

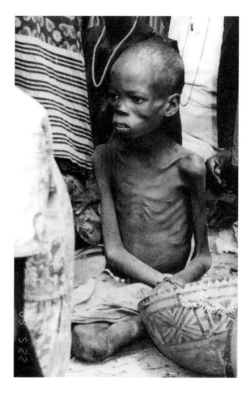

In 1993, after twenty-nine years of marriage, I found myself divorced, at loose ends, not knowing what to do. Out of the blue, I received a call from World Vision, a Christian relief organization, asking whether I would go to work with refugees in Angola. Despite my attempts in the years since, I have never been able to solve the mystery of how they got my name. That call led to four trips with World Vision, two to Angola, one to Kosovo, and one in 1998 to Sudan, to which Fairview contributed.

In Sudan, we automatically gave worm medicine and antibiotics to all the children we saw. While considered poor medical practice in the West, this is deemed appropriate treatment by both the United Nations and UNICEF in areas where prolonged malnutrition not only leaves weakened systems prone to infection, but masks the symptoms as well. We gave out vitamin A—its deficiency indicated by the ulcers on many eyes—and vaccinations, still a novelty to many. Any unexplained fever we treated with malarial drugs, this mosquito-borne illness being so common.

The major goal of World Vision centers on bringing starving people back from the brink. Nearly all the Sudanese suffer hunger, but as a necessary method of triaging, only those demonstrating a less than 70 percent weight to height ratio (African standards) will be admitted to a feeding center. After months of malnutrition and under 70 percent of its optimum weight, the body ceases to function properly and refuses normal food, which is thrown up if ingested. We give these patients an oral rehydration solution for one or two days, one painstaking tablespoon at a time. From there we graduate to recovery milk, a powder fortified with vitamins, minerals, vegetable oil, and sugar and mixed with boiled water. When patients can handle this, we move on to a fortified soy/corn mush, graduating finally to beans and other real food.

The hierarchy of starvation outside the feeding center dictates that men get available food first, then women, then children. Those most endangered are the two-to-four-year-olds. Older children scramble for anything edible; younger ones breastfeed. The in-betweeners lose out.

We allow one adult or sibling with each child. Out of necessity we feed that person, too. We can't just give food to the children. A few years ago I would not have believed it, but with my own eyes I have seen: when malnutrition is long and severe, when death becomes a constant companion, the drive for self-preservation supersedes even maternal instinct, and mothers will eat the food meant for the children. All of these mothers have buried children. When asked how many children they have, they will list first the dead and then the living. Some families have buried a child or two on the way to the feeding center.

The United States boasts three and a half million miles of paved road. The entire country of Sudan claims only some twenty-seven hundred. The vast majority of these roads run through the Arab (northern) two-thirds of the country rather than the south. There are no roads of any kind to Theit, a collection of mud huts known as *tukals* that have a hole for a door and thatch for a roof. Next to these we set up our feeding center at the edge of the desert. The news spread by word of mouth, and over vast expanses of roadless, parched terrain, the people came. Some of them owned a piece of clothing, which they wore; often the children went naked. Some carried a tin can for water, but none had housing or food. They had survived by eating grass, roasting rats, and boiling cowhide—a sea of dispossessed and possessionless specters trying to stay alive for one more day. It's hard to accept the fact that people can exist like this.

We were organized to handle up to three hundred fifty people but ended up feeding fifteen hundred who camped out in the open among the bugs, snakes, and scorpions. I slept in a tent with protective mosquito netting dividing me from the mosquitoes, spiders, and other creepy crawlies. I used a latrine consisting of a hole in the ground, drank tea and ate cornflakes with water for breakfast, and invariably had goat for dinner. My workday began at 6:30 or 7:00 A.M. when the feeding center opened. It continued through the 120-degree midday, and ended sixteen or eighteen hours later.

Not all of the children made it. If their weight registered at least 55 percent of what it should have been for their height, usually we could save them. Under that, we found them too far gone to bring back. Not only had their body devoured its own fat but also its muscle. Metabolic and brain damage had proceeded too far to be reversed, and the end proved inevitable.

Why would I leave America to go to a forsaken place like Sudan? asked one of the translators. I am a Christian, I replied, and in this way I can share my faith. I've had a comfortable life, and it's time for me to do something for somebody else.

I find myself bothered by the amount of waste in the United States. Material things attract me less than they once did. Seeing what I saw in Sudan has provided a wonderful antidote to self-pity. My problems seem inconsequential in comparison to the daily struggle for survival I witnessed in so many hungry faces. I am eternally thankful that my children and grandchildren are all happy and healthy. Their fate could have been so different had they been born elsewhere.

I recognize that to a large extent, we operated a revolving door, discharging patients once they reached 80 percent of their optimum weight in order to make room for others. They often returned, on the verge of starvation again in a few days or weeks.

I did what I could. I'll never forget working in a sea of hundreds of children—bedless, chairless, sitting or lying listlessly on the ground, a few lucky enough to rest under the shade of a tree. No horseplay, no yelling, none of the restlessness we associate with children. After a few days of feeding, the area became notably noisier as much-needed nutrition turned them, for a while, into the happy and playful children they would have been had they been born somewhere else.

Guatemala

HELPS International

Adding Another Dimension

"What becomes of people such as these when groups like ours aren't there?"

MIKE MANDT

PHARMACIST

I didn't know what I was getting into that first trip.

A local doctor had received my name as someone who might be interested in going with a HELPS team to Guatemala. He himself had nothing to do with the team but agreed to ask if I would go. He stopped me one day as our paths crossed in the hall. Since the team was one person short, they really needed me, he said—to leave in two weeks. Unbelievably, I agreed.

I flew alone from Minnesota to meet a group of strangers in Houston and continue on to Guatemala. From Guatemala City, the village of Nebaj lay some sixty miles up a beautiful but sometimes treacherous mountain road. Our bus climbed steep hills, making hairpin turns on loose gravel until the road degenerated into little more than a path for the last fifteen miles. This bumpy ride took ten hours.

We set up our pharmacy in one of the hospitals, built, as I understand it, with U.S. government help but left largely unused due to staffing problems. We brought our own medicines, food, and cots and slept in the hospital, men in one area and women in another. HELPS provided additional food as well as cooks who worked in the hospital kitchen. During our eight-day stay, we left the hospital compound only once to go into town.

I entered a different pharmaceutical world. I had nothing familiar but the reference book I had brought. No computer. No technology. I wrote labels by hand. Accustomed to having access to anything I needed, I found myself limited by the medicines we had brought—basic antibiotics, anti-inflammatory drugs, pain killers. Watching the supply dwindle as the week went by, I asked doctors' permission to make substitutions from the little that remained.

To think I had gotten there all because of a chance meeting in the hall.

I appreciated the lack of status-consciousness within HELPS. Surgeons, cooks, mechanics, and janitors worked on an equal basis, providing a true example of teamwork with no hierarchy. For the most part, the interpreters triaged. They picked possible candidates for surgery, who were then further categorized by the surgeons. (The types of surgeons vary with each HELPS group.) The hospital offered only an X-ray, pharmacy, and two operating rooms, thereby limiting the number of surgeries possible. Postsurgical patients spent the night together in a single recovery room.

Guatemalan HELPS representatives had done their publicity job well. Outside the gated compound, lines of hundreds formed as people from other villages walked in to be seen. Organizers allowed those with normal complaints to see doctors as space and time allowed. Those we could not examine on a particular day either returned to their home or slept outside to wait for the next day's clinic.

I found myself hard-pressed to keep up in the pharmacy. Since the people's work is so physically hard, many of their visits dealt with nonspecific complaints of body aches remediable by simple Advil. Nevertheless, filling the prescriptions of the physicians, seeing one patient after another, and giving everyone vitamins and de-worming medicine made for exhausting ten-hour days, even with another pharmacist and two helpers.

Language barriers and illiteracy combined to slow the pace. In many cases, we had to relay dosage explanations through two interpreters, English to Spanish, then Spanish to Ixil, the local Mayan language. For the illiterate, we resorted to such tactics as drawing a sun for "Take one in the morning" and a moon for "Take one at night."

Dispensing medications forms a necessary part of patient care in both the United States and Guatemala. Working within the four walls of a pharmacy, however, leaves the pharmacist unaware of the effects of the medications. He or she rarely sees the sometimes dramatic results that the patient's physician does. Yet once in a while, we hear about them.

Parents brought in a little boy with congenital cataracts that had denied him the gift of sight. A team surgeon removed the cataracts, leaving the child bandaged overnight. The next day, team members held a stuffed toy in front of the boy as they carefully uncovered his eyes. Unbandaged, the little one made a gleeful grab at the first object he had ever been able to see.

Another dramatic incident occurred not during work at the hospital but on the day the team went into town. On market days, sellers offer beautifully woven textiles in stalls next to cooking utensils, crockery, tomatoes, beans, corn, eggs, chickens, or a half of beef hanging from a meat hook in the eighty-degree heat. With no stores as we know them, the market becomes the equivalent of a mall.

We wandered about, absorbing the local culture. The men of Guatemalan villages can appear indistinguishable, all wearing dark pants, a white shirt, and boots. The women, however, dress in locally woven cloth of their particular village. Those of Nebaj wear red and gold skirts, a blouse, vest, and scarf or hat. In a larger city you can immediately pick out a woman of Nebaj by the color of her skirt, just as a woman of another village will identify herself by a different color pattern.

It was near the church that team members found the little girl. Perhaps ten or twelve years of age, literally purple from hypoxia, with clubbed fingers possibly caused by the same condition, she suffered from a congenital heart defect. The surgery to correct this lay beyond the possibilities of our team. Not giving up, we got the larger HELPS organization involved. HELPS convinced the Guatemalan government, with which it stands on good terms, to send a military helicopter to take the child and her mother to Guatemala City. As the helicopter landed on the soccer field, villagers chattered about how good it was to see a military helicopter flying overhead without shooting at them. War memories remain fresh.

A subsequent team of American surgeons took the piece necessary to repair the child's heart with them to Guatemala, performing the surgery that saved her life. The next year, various team members and I headed off in the back of a pickup truck to see her. Out of the same little house near the church stepped a smiling figure, tall and slim, her once purple skin returned to its natural olive color. The little girl we had found dying was growing and blossoming.

Those of us who have gone on a mission trip know that the work proves harder than anything we do on our regular job. Yet we return time and again. We sweat, sleep on a cot, eat canned food, have access to minimal supplies, receive no pay, give up vacation, and pay out of our own pockets to go—and still claim to be of sound mind.

I enjoy both types of vacations—kicking back and lying on the beach *and* helping humanity. The second proves more fulfilling—adventure with an added dimension. Mission travel resets my priorities. From the hustle and bustle of life in the States, trying to climb the career ladder to the next rung, I find I have to go back and get another dose of *simple* living. The evening news on any channel you choose shows chaos. In Nebaj, everyone knows the neighbors, doors have no locks, and no one has much to steal anyway. I wouldn't switch, yet it does me good to go there.

These experiences force me to think about life in general. In the United States, we consider everything either fixable or blamable. The poor in Guatemala accept that not everything has a solution. Bad things just happen. I find the Guatemalans the sweetest people I could ever imagine. They don't complain, although they have nothing. Here we have everything, yet we find fault.

I also contrast the medical possibilities we have available. While I could not get a heart bypass at the hospital where I work, I could drive sixty miles to another and get one. In Nebaj, HELPS team doctors performed cesarean sections on two women. Had we not been there, these women would have faced the option of a ten-hour bus ride into Guatemala City. That assumes, of course, that they could get the money and have the time to go. These mountain people take risks if and when they travel to the city. Unused to traffic (I saw no personal cars in Nebaj), they prove frequent victims of pedestrian accidents. In the United States, we have a single culture. In Guatemala, between the mountains and the cities, there are two.

My wife and I had traveled extensively before we adopted two Honduran children. Someday I want to take them back to Central America to show them where they came from. They have moved from a dirt-floored hut to the Mall of America.

As to the usefulness of mission trips, I think of the "widows' houses" built in Guatemala for those who lost both husband and home in the thirty-six-year civil war. I consider the beneficial effect of the antiparasitic medicine given to all. Some of the worm cases doctors saw can only be qualified as awful. Even if patients get worms again, we have made them healthy for a while. The sixty vitamins or thirty Advil will run out, but the goodwill and trust we have built will remain. The goodwill extends beyond the personal and into governmental levels. On my last trip, our group visited the presidential palace by invitation and received the personal greetings of the president and first lady.

We only go for a week. Are the time and expense worth it? I remember the two women with the C-sections. I think of the little boy seeing a stuffed toy for the first time. I visualize a dying girl made healthy again because a team member found her. I ask myself, what becomes of people such as these during the other weeks of the year, when groups like ours aren't there? I think I know what happens.

Bangladesh

Lutheran Health Care / Bangladesh

In a Heartbeat

"You're not any good to anyone if you're dead."

MONICA LINDLIEF

REGISTERED NURSE

The unknown had always fascinated me. In particular, I found myself drawn by the aura of Eastern culture. When a planned trip to India failed to work out, I called an executive at Lutheran Health Care/ Bangladesh. I found him both informative and personally excited about the Bangladesh project. I left that phone conversation convinced that Bangladesh would be a good choice, and the more I learned, the more comfortable I felt.

I would fly alone to Dhaka, the capital, and from there travel by a combination of car and various ferries to the village of Dumki. My job there would be threefold: teaching local maternity/childhood hospital nurses three days a week (something comparable to in-service here), attending to the in-hospital patients, and making a twice-weekly trip into rural villages to take care of health problems there. The plan seemed forthright and uncomplicated. I prepared for a ten-month stay.

At the beginning, I lived in a primitive house of cement floors and walls in which a single bed graced my lackluster room. Employed by LHCB, a caretaker family of three cooked and cleaned, sharing a single small room at the back while I lived in the front. They served me a version of lentil soup over rice, curry and fish, or curry and chicken. For supper, they attempted to make what they thought an American must like—grilled cheese sandwiches, soup, hamburgers, and spaghetti with tomatoes. While these well-intended dishes didn't always reflect our concept of the same items, the accompanying vegetables and fruits never failed to rate a ten.

Table utensils did not exist. (I wanted to experience a new culture, I reminded myself.) Everything was eaten with the fingers of the right hand, the left being considered unsanitary. From what I saw, eating did not allow for lefties, who of necessity learned to use their right hand.

Every day I drank four liters of water, sweating it off in the stifling heat. I ate until I felt stuffed, yet found my caretakers daily urging me to eat more. I never saw what they ate. Despite my feeling that I must be putting on weight, I had lost ten pounds by the time I came back.

When the water in the house well ran dry, LHCB moved me to a guesthouse in the hospital area. Also built of cement, it offered four rooms, each with a bathroom and hot shower when the electricity worked. The rooms contained lanterns and candles for the two to four hours a day that the electricity went out. While we would consider this lifestyle "camping out," it rated high compared to the conditions in other houses.

Sponsorship of the hospital by Lutheran Health Care/ Bangladesh and the Evangelical Lutheran Church/Division of Global Missions undoubtedly explained the prevalence of Christian nurses. I marveled at their focus as they demonstrated a strong faith within a Muslim culture in which they formed a small minority. They took it in stride, having known nothing else, and offered daily morning devotions from 8:00 to 8:10 each morning. Hindus and Muslims formed a smaller part of the staff, members of all three religions working together in harmony for the benefit of the patients.

Mondays, Wednesdays, and Fridays—through an interpreter—I gave lectures and talked with the nurses, speaking on universal precautions, asthma, pneumonia, and other conditions I saw. Most nurses' English had never progressed beyond the basic level. The hospital was working to remedy the lack of understanding of a language in which so much medical material is written, offering English language classes for an hour twice a week. Doctors, nurses, and patients communicated in Bengali, using whoever could speak best as interpreter for me. I, in the meantime, attended language classes to learn Bengali.

Not only language, but nursing remained basic. I saw two cesareans done under drip-flow anesthesia while a nurse visually monitored the patient's respiration, there being no machines. There was no portable suction, no X-ray, no oxygen. I will say that the nurses did what they could with what they had, wearing sterile gowns behind the covered screened windows of the enclosed operating room. The ward consisted of a single room with six beds separated by rarely used curtains.

A twenty-five-year-old woman—out of the ordinary in that she was attending graduate school—came in to have her first baby. Speaking moderate English, she became one of the patients I got to know best. I marveled at her gratefulness for the time I spent talking with her. Invariably, she ended our conversations with, "Thank you for speaking with me." She insisted that I be present when she gave birth, as indeed I was. When I returned at night to check on her and the baby, I met her husband. The two had one request in common: they wanted me to name the baby. Taken by surprise, I stammered that this was their choice, something special for them. Yet I felt honored. Who was I to name their baby? When they persisted, I promised to think about it, but they ended up choosing the name themselves.

Four and a half months later, I received a letter from this woman and realized that I had formed a bond I hadn't expected to make in so short a time. In return, I sent her a picture of my family. When my church made baby blankets for the hospital, I made sure there was an extra one for her.

On the days I wasn't lecturing or working at the hospital, I accompanied local doctors and nurses as they took mobile clinics to rural areas. There we worked for the most part on prenatal care and cases of tuberculosis, asthma, and other respiratory diseases. The group included a lab technician, a record keeper, a doctor, a pharmacist, me, and a cooler-sized crate of medicines. To some areas we drove; to others, we drove partway, then continued downriver by boat. In general, we stayed at a site for three or four hours, during which time there was a mandatory break at 10:00 or 11:00 A.M. for hot tea from a thermos. In the heat, hot tea seemed the last thing I wanted to drink, and I fought to keep a straight face at this incongruous legacy of the British, who once held sway in the area.

So my routine continued. One Monday, a pharmacist—a fellow Minnesotan no less—arrived. He was looking forward to two months of work as I looked forward to another eight. Then, in a heartbeat, our world turned upside down.

At 8:30 the night of Tuesday, September 11, Bijoy, the president of the Bangladeshi arm of LHCB, phoned with the news—just minutes old in the United States—that the New York World Trade Center had been attacked. Subsequent reflection has left me impressed with his handling of the situation. He remained calm, making us feel safe. Nevertheless, we remained acutely aware that we Americans could be

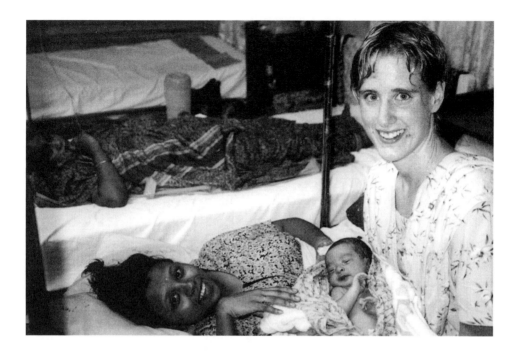

vulnerable as well. We received no other information until the BBC broadcast came on at 9:00 P.M., then nothing further until 3:00 P.M. the next day. I phoned home to get more news. As a precaution, Bijoy sent more police to Dumki.

On Thursday morning, considering that we might have to be shipped out, he sent us back to Dhaka to be near the airport. No one had a clue if and when the United States might retaliate. We remained at the Dhaka guesthouse for a little less than a week, during which time the Bangladeshis gave us their condolences. "We're sorry for what happened to your country," one after another repeated to us. Yet I felt that they didn't really grasp the immensity of the situation, the seriousness of the threat to the United States, or the impact of so many deaths. This last I could understand, death being so common in Bangladesh. Meanwhile, even as we received the condolences of individuals, the

Dhaka papers were quoting a Malaysian who had referred to the tragedy as "sad, but what the United States had coming."

We met with other Americans at the embassy. Government officials never ordered us to leave. They did point out, however, the thousands and thousands of dollars it would cost the Air Force to come and get us out should something happen and we become trapped. The official analysis of our situation boiled down to five words: "We cannot guarantee your safety."

It was hard to switch gears after so much planning and hard work, but playing the hero was going to accomplish nothing. You're not any good to anyone if you're dead. We packed and came home, my ten months ending after two. The pharmacist had worked one day.

The people of the United States and Bangladesh inhabit two incomparable worlds. In Bangladesh, everything takes longer. If people don't accomplish as much as we in a day, they lose no sleep over it. The attitude is more relaxed: we'll do what we can, we'll do our best, things will work out. Coming back here makes it hard not to fall into our normal rush-rush mode. Nevertheless, I try to step back, appreciate what I have, and remember that I don't always need something more or better.

I had wanted to find a medical mission where I could use my nursing. LHCB proved a good fit. I met people I never would have encountered had I stayed home. I saw their lives and learned what was important to them. The Bangladeshis are probably the most gracious people I've ever encountered. They have almost nothing yet are profoundly thankful for what they do have. I realize how blessed I am with what I have. I wanted to give something back to others, yet I gained far more than I gave.

I come from a small town where people in my home church contributed generously toward my going to a faraway place they would never see. I went with their blessing, their money, and their prayers. I also worked overtime, saved my own money, and applied for grants to enable me to go for ten months. It made it all the more frustrating to have to come home so soon when I had worked so hard to get there.

Back at Fairview-University Medical Center, I'm applying to graduate school to study anesthesia. One of my main goals is undertaking two-week mission trips twice a year. Specifically, I want to return to Bangladesh. In Dumki, I never considered my life in danger, but that was before the United States retaliated for the terrorist attacks. If and when the embassy declares it safe, I'll go back—in a heartbeat.

Nicaragua

Witness for Peace

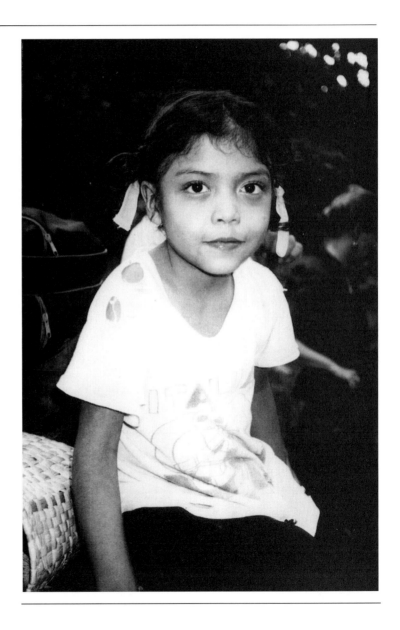

Little Time and Much to Do

"I find myself compelled to live in a way that feels worthwhile."

DAVID HARRIS

RETIRED SURGEON

In northern Nicaragua in 1998, rains from Hurricane Mitch filled the empty crater of a volcano to the point where it burst. The resulting rush of floodwaters hit the little town of Posoltega, drowning two thousand people in the space of an hour. Of the remaining fourteen thousand or so inhabitants, most had lost homes. Many had lost someone they loved, and numerous individuals were injured. So it was that my team and I found ourselves—several nurses, a psychologist, two physician's assistants, two young Nicaraguan guides, and two doctors— walking not into a town but into a camp of refugees.

As the surviving townspeople slept together on the concrete floors of schools or other remaining buildings, we encountered a lot of respiratory and gastrointestinal illnesses. Many who had come through the flood alive suffered from anxiety and depression, what we would call post-traumatic stress syndrome. Cholera, always feared when people crowd together under nonhygienic conditions, never appeared. For this I credit the efforts of the regional director of the Public Health Service, who had traveled immediately to the site and instituted programs to bring in bottled water and remove sewage. The public health workers appeared exhausted but did their job.

They told us where to help, and we went, visiting different refugee groupings each day. We gave immunizations provided by the Nicaraguan government and shared the antibiotic, antidiarrheal, and other medicines we had brought. We also dispensed numerous tranquilizers, as many of the survivors had lost children or parents. The psychologist among us organized games to distract the children. Altogether, we tried to give people the sense that they could reshape meaningful lives.

In a situation like this, the need is so great that any amount of care you give seems insignificant. This is true in nonemergency situations as well. As a result, I tend to work more with health education rather than actual care.

Over the past sixteen years, I have packed my bags and traveled to Central America seventeen times. On some occasions, I have taught surgical techniques to eager Nicaraguan medical students and house staff. On others, I have participated in medical symposia in Nicaragua, El Salvador, or Guatemala, where in 1992 I took a group of doctors and nurses to run a clinic. In 1998, as described, I contributed to the emergency help that was offered after Hurricane Mitch.

During my trips to Nicaragua, I have learned more than which diseases and health problems plague the population. I have learned of the atrocities that went on during the 1980s' civil war. I observed the 1990 Nicaraguan elections as a representative of Witness for Peace and became part of its board of directors early in the same decade. This faith-based organization works to promote justice for oppressed peoples in Latin America and the Caribbean—in Chiapas (Mexico),

Guatemala, Colombia, Haiti, and Nicaragua, to name a few places. Members work to change American foreign policy in cases where it causes human suffering.

In the 1980s, our government funded the Contras to overthrow the Sandinistas in Nicaragua. Few people outside of Nicaragua took the resulting plight of the people into account as the Contras murdered schoolteachers and health workers, burned clinics, and scattered parts of the country with U.S.-made land mines. In 1987, a health group visited with the American ambassador in Managua. "The Contras have made some mistakes," he admitted, "but they're not doing those things anymore. We've controlled that." The very next day, in the town of Jinotega, we saw a funeral for two boys shot by the Contras while carting shoes to market.

Americans see national interest and national security as abstract concepts. I have witnessed the individual suffering caused, in my opinion, by U.S. foreign policies. Amazingly, everywhere I went, people had no difficulty distinguishing between what our government was doing and what we as individual Americans were trying to do.

So what did we accomplish in Nicaragua? I would say that our impact on people's health and well-being amounted to little, considering the enormity of the task. Nevertheless, I have always felt that you have to try. If you do nothing, nothing results. Something, no matter how small, is still something accomplished. Furthermore, apart from addressing health concerns, we made friends. More than the party the Nicaraguans threw for us, more than the certificate of service, the heartfelt gratefulness of individuals and our pleasure in making friends measured the worthiness of this undertaking. Making friends and sharing hope may be the best thing I've done.

I do not consider myself either a pessimist or an optimist, but these trips have changed my life. It may not be possible to do a lot in

this world, but I have to do what I can. I find myself compelled to live in a way that feels worthwhile. There remains so much to do and not a lot of time left to do it.

I have gradually seen my efforts turn from healthcare to human rights. Really, the two intertwine, and the connection becomes more recognized daily. Last year, the University of Minnesota held a weeklong symposium on health and human rights. Poor people lack access to education, one of the cornerstones of basic hygiene and health. Women in many countries never expect the same from life as men. They remain sexually exploited both legally and illegally, often becoming unwitting victims of AIDS and other sexually transmitted diseases.

You don't improve human rights and healthcare without getting involved in political issues. For my part, I talk mostly to grassroots participants rather than politicians, although I have done both. My experience with foreign human rights abuses has induced me to involve myself with American problems. Largely as a result of these experiences, I have become a member of the Red Wing Human Rights Commission. Along with others, I tackle local issues of racism; housing, workplace, and school inadequacies; and inequities regarding gender, sexual orientation, and disability. Having recently been elected to my local school board, I hope to work on an even bigger human rights gap in our society—children's loss of connection with a safe, reliable, loving adult. Such satisfying work makes my life rich.

My foreign travels came to a standstill two years ago when my mother, diagnosed with Alzheimer's, came to live with us. She died recently, and I'm thinking of Latin America again.

I know I won't find myself alone in my efforts. To maintain faith, you have to rely on others and trust in the common spirit that moves among us. It need not have a name. I define it simply as something more than just us.

On my first trip to Central America, I found myself alone on a plane full of non-English-speaking travelers. I knew no Spanish. After the initial moments of misgiving, I felt sudden relief at the realization that I was powerless. Everything lay out of my hands. The comfortable feeling about life and death that descended upon me during that flight has never left. I have a deep-seated, if nontraditional, religious faith. I have led a lucky life blessed with good health and filled with adventures. I have spent forty-four years with a woman I love, being blessed with three wonderful children. I could die happy today, having lived a full life. If I don't die today, that's even better, as I still have plenty to do.

Guatemala

Common Hope (formerly God Child Project)

Nothing but Themselves

"I wish everyone could experience this poverty and see how happy these people are, even though they have nothing but themselves."

JAN PALMER

LICENSED PRACTICAL NURSE

Not only had I never traveled to a developing country before, I had never even boarded a plane. The turbulence frightened me, like bumping over a dirt road with no landscape by which to measure speed or distance. I insisted on an aisle seat and spent some anxious moments regretting my promise to help with the God Child Project.

A friend of mine who worked in the surgical unit of a large hospital had talked me into it. The agency name came from the group's original purpose, sponsoring children at $30 a month to cover all of their medical expenses and half of their families'. The children had to remain in school in order to be eligible. From this beginning, the organization had expanded to sending medical teams. Due to the confusion with another group called God's Child, the organization changed its name to Common Hope in early 2000. Maintaining offices in St. Paul, Minnesota, and Antigua, Guatemala, it works with the Berhharst Clinic and Hospital in Chimaltenango to set up surgeries for medical teams.

The Common Hope compound in Antigua not only has a nursing school, but also offers adult workshops for the general population—woodworking, agricultural improvement, chicken breeding, sewing—as well as a medical and dental clinic. One young man I know talked his parent (from Switzerland) into coming to do dental work for a couple of weeks. After four years, they are still there. It's easy to get hooked on this.

Our team of twenty-five or so stays in a hotel with cold running water. We eat our meals in the screened porch of the nursing school, where three cooks squeeze orange juice and prepare tortillas, beans, rice, chicken, vegetables, and bananas. I am a vegetarian, and after witnessing the conditions in which meat hangs or sits in unrefrigerated open-air markets in Guatemala, I see even less reason to eat meat there.

Throughout the year, the local doctors screen their everyday patients and pick those among the poor who can most use our services. Although we do see other cases—one of which I will relate—we specialize in cleft palate and cleft lip surgery for children. A speech therapist accompanies us. We also see hernias in adults and do burn repair on anyone. The preselected patients pay the equivalent of $8 to cover their surgical lab work but are charged nothing further.

Due to the overall level of poverty, the local doctors offer no painkillers beyond Tylenol and no general anesthesia, lacking the requisite equipment. We bring our own equipment, including instruments.

Of the four small rooms in the clinic, one is reserved for the local doctors, who continue to see patients, while the other three are ceded to us. Conditions being primitive, we improvise. Shower curtain hooks fastened onto overhead pipes serve to carry IV tubes. Shoe organizer

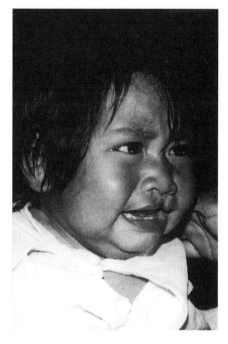

bags nailed to walls hold small pieces of equipment. The anesthesia machine we vent through the open window. Concrete blocks raise the operating table to gringo height, while cotton sheets hung above the surgery area keep bugs from falling on top. Cots lined up against the walls turn one cubicle into a recovery room, where children lie until half-awake. Their parents then take them to the adjoining room for a few hours until their IV is finished and they have stabilized. All in all, it works.

Due to the limited facilities of local doctors, patients with severe injuries often receive inadequate treatment or none at all. At our request, a frightened twelve-year-old girl with the prettiest brown eyes demonstrated the limited degree to which she was able to straighten her heavily scarred right arm. The entire right side of her little body, down to her waist, carried the marks of old burns. The arm, most affected, had been so damaged that it could be only partially extended, as no grafting or reconstructive surgery had ever been done.

Children go to work young in developing countries, the boys helping their fathers in the fields or in the streets, the girls helping their mothers with their chores. Seven years earlier, the fire from the open cookstove in the girl's house had caught her dress as she tended the meal, setting her on fire. Presumably, nothing more than Tylenol was made available to her in that horrible time.

There remained nothing we could do for the scarring, but we could cut the twisted flesh of her arm and reconstruct it so that she could fully extend it. We tried to insert the IV needle into a vein and failed. As we tried again, tears began streaming down her frightened face. No sound came from her mouth, but her little body racked with silent sobs as she did her best to remain stoic.

The stoicism and pain tolerance of these people amazes me. I work in an emergency room in the States, but I see as many sore throats and hangnails as anything else. We are truly a whining and ungrateful society. The Guatemalans, on the other hand, may wait ten or twelve years to see a doctor, if they do at all, and they are so grateful for any care they get. They ask for nothing, yet demonstrate unbridled enthusiasm over a few Tylenol, a little blanket for their baby, or a garage sale castoff. We make it a habit to give dime-store jewelry, Matchbox cars, or other small gifts to the siblings of the children we treat so that they feel included. Their joy at receiving these trinkets knows no bounds. I wish everyone could experience this poverty and see how happy these people are, even though they have nothing but themselves.

One day, along with a social worker and another team member, I visited the child my teammate sponsored. The family of five shared a single bedroom with three beds and a small dresser. The other room of the house had a table, a bench, one chair, and an open cook pit. That was all. The mother, who worked as a maid for a wealthier townsperson, had swept the dirt smooth in her outer yard so that it would look nice for our coming, which constituted a major event in their lives.

This work thrills me. My husband, while he has no desire to go himself, supports my efforts and is proud of me. My Minnesota coworkers help me collect blankets, sheets, soaps, toothpaste, and school supplies to make life a little better for the less fortunate in Guatemala.

I grew up poor. My father was an alcoholic, and I know what it is to not have enough food. I live frugally in a simple house and don't spend much except on my hobbies. Yet I am wealthy compared to these humble poor. What are bugs and cold water for a few days out of my entire life, if, by enduring this, I can make their lives a little better?

I find myself comfortable with Guatemalans. I like beans and tortillas. I have washed my clothes on the rocks in the river, impressing the local women with our kinship as we perform the same timeless task. These people have little other contact with Americans. Our actions and kindnesses, as Americans and as individuals, are not forgotten.

Kazakhstan, Mongolia

Cornerstone Church, Twin Cities Chinese Christian Church

Toward a Lasting Impact

"The medical schools take their students straight out of ninth grade.
After a six-year program with no residency training,
they turn out full-fledged doctors, age twenty-one."

BEN LEO

FAMILY PRACTITIONER

I was born in a developing country—Taiwan—from which my parents
brought me to the United States when I was five. They pursued the
American dream, rising from poverty through industriousness to the
middle class. Yet they never forgot where they came from, bringing me
up on remembrances of a world different from my comfortable
American life.

I took chemistry as a college major, realizing as I matured that
sociology or anthropology would have suited me better. I wanted to
help people. Once I decided on family practice, I knew that sooner or
later I would become involved in international medicine. After residency, I remained uncertain about whether to take on international
missions full time or not. Various short-term missions provided an
ideal alternative.

Along with my parents' stories and those I had read about the medicine, struggles, and challenges in developing countries, my faith proved a strong component of my desire to serve. It was in church that I first learned of opportunities overseas, but it was through a chance encounter that I went on my first mission trip. Through a reception-ist at a Fairview clinic, I found out about a former pastor (her hus-band) who led such medical trips. I left her my name. Four months later, having heard nothing, I had all but given up. By strange coinci-dence, I ran into the receptionist and her husband at a Chinese restaurant. Two doctor friends were eating with me that night. All three of us ended up going to Kazakhstan for an entire month.

There we planned a holistic offering of physical and spiritual attention, depending on patients' needs. We worked with a group of Kazakh natives, Americans, and Australians doing full-time medical work in this former republic of the Soviet Union. The Kazakhs told tales about the first several years after Kazakhstan broke away from the Soviet Union. People stood in line for hours for the limited food available when the old system no longer supplied it. From what I saw, supply still lagged behind demand. More products were available in the capital, but poor distribution or lack of products relegated coun-try people to a subsistence living from their animals' meat and milk. These rural people lived a seminomadic existence in dwellings called yurts, round canvas tents covered with canvas and yak skin.

Kazakh independence led also to a resurgence of nationalism, the national language reverting from Russian to Kazakh. This caused some difficulties, as decades of children had gone through a school system run in Russian. Nevertheless, the country was determined to return to its roots.

Religion likewise saw something of a revival. Kazakhs knew that they once were Muslim, but years of Communism had all but eliminated open practice. The people wore Western dress, showing none of the outer trappings of Islam (veiled or covered women) so obvious in some societies. The lack of medical modesty, in fact, surprised us. Women automatically pulled up their tops to let us hear their heart or lungs. They had been so accustomed by Soviet doctors.

Medically speaking, we saw the same things as in the States. The difference lay in the greater number of advanced diseases made worse by neglect. Untreated high blood pressure and diabetes proved particularly noteworthy.

Our itinerary encompassed clinical work and house calls, including one to the home of our interpreter's father. Most city dwellers lived in apartments, characterless concrete structures that were six to eight stories high with small windows. Each building looked like its neighbor. This family, however, had a house. Considered middle-class, the concrete structure sat on a yard of trampled dirt behind a ten-foot wooden fence. All too aware of the high crime rate, the family—like many—owned dogs as an extra protection. The house contained a small kitchen and a bedroom as well as a living or family room in which the old man lay covered on a cot.

Typical of many born at home during a time when no records were kept, he was unsure of his age but might have been in his sixties. Having suffered a massive stroke that resulted in paralysis of one side of his body, he nevertheless had no medicine for his high blood pressure.

There wasn't much I could do for him. I suggested aspirin, of which I left a good supply. I considered blood pressure medicine, but decided against it. My limited stock would not last him long, and he had no way of getting more. If such medicine is suddenly stopped, blood pressure may rebound higher than ever. Further, I knew that in areas where medicine is hard to come by, people (besides using medicine we might have used forty years ago) tend to use it sparingly and

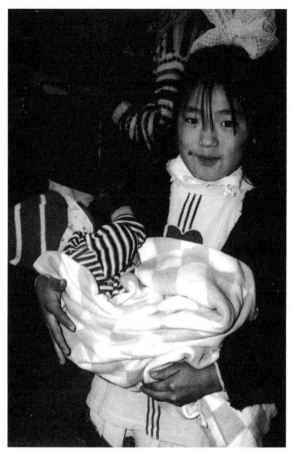

irregularly, often nullifying its effect.

This incident and others like it led me to conclude that picking a few people and giving them a year's worth of medicine had more merit than giving a week's worth to a multitude. Similar incidents also made me aware of the great need not only for medicines, but for supplies. (Doctors had insufficient sterile gloves, of necessity reusing what they had. Dressings and other items that we take for granted stood in short supply as well.) Nutritional diversity—particularly from vegetables—proved a further need. For the month of our stay, we talked frequently about what we would eat when we returned to the States. The unanimous vote went for a huge salad. Our food in Kazakhstan consisted mainly of mutton and mare's milk. We only saw two or three kinds of vegetables on the whole trip.

Conditions proved worse in the prison we visited in the northern part of the country. One of the three highest security prisons in the former Soviet Union, it housed murderers, rapists, and the like. Widely held rumors told how prison gang members used to kill each other with some regularity until a local man started a Christian prison fellowship that changed the character of the place within a year. This attracted some of the guards and even the warden to Christianity.

We had hoped to treat the inmates, but the prison doctor sabotaged this effort—embarrassed, we assumed, for us to see how little he had to work with. He did allow us to examine selected prisoners but not to treat them. A typical cell contained a single cot on which one of two inmates would sleep while the other slept on the concrete floor. A simple hole in the floor served as a latrine, while a small window fifteen feet up the wall gave some light. Six-inch-thick metal doors blocked the front of every cell.

Four doctors and the team leader entered each cell accompanied by a guard. If the cowering and cringing of prisoners on seeing the guard had not convinced us of the physical abuse of inmates, the frequent rib and chest injuries we saw definitely did. The inmate had fallen off a horse, a guard responded to one of our questioning looks. Right.

A fourth of the prisoners had tuberculosis, a fact we had guessed beforehand that caused us some trepidation about entering the prison in the first place. We decided to pray about it and felt a strong urging to go despite the risks. Because of its high resistance, tuberculosis is normally treated with three or four medicines over a protracted period. The tiny prison clinic had no X-ray machine and only one or two antitubercular medicines, which it dispensed for a very limited time due to the short supply. At the conclusion of our visit, we left all our medicines with the prison doctor.

I accomplished little, medically speaking, during my month in Kazakhstan. But I gave a lot and gained a lot in terms of relationships, be it with the local doctors, the interpreter, or an occasional patient. Our efforts, I decided, should best be seen as bolstering the work of those who stay rather than making a permanent difference on our own.

The people of eastern Kazakhstan and western Mongolia are one and the same. Attracted to the idea of going where few people have traveled, I went with a team to Mongolia in 1997. (This trip, besides introducing me to Mongolia, introduced me to my future wife.)

We worked with the Mongolian Good Neighbor Society, an organization holding goals similar to mine: to improve the economy, teach health education and technological skills, and demonstrate such basics as growing one's own vegetables. Our goal as a team focused on forming relationships with Mongolian doctors. We brought a few medicines as well as a donation of stethoscopes, which we raffled to doctors attending the medical seminars we offered. We made certain that some went to those who had traveled the farthest. Those receiving a stethoscope promised to donate their old one to someone who had none.

Mongolian doctors earn about $25 a month, less than an interpreter or a cabdriver. Yet I found them totally dedicated to their patients, their frequent medical mistakes due not to lack of caring but to lack of education or experience. Many had no formal medical training, having learned what they knew through an apprenticeship to another doctor. We soon realized that many didn't really know how to examine patients or even how to take proper histories.

As a result, that first year I ran into situations that left me angry and frustrated. In one village, for example, hospital doctors had admitted a woman thirty-three weeks pregnant who complained of kidney pain. Now, Mongolians refer to all back pain as kidney pain, and Mongolian doctors often go along with this. For seven days, they had been giving this woman, who was suffering nothing more than the normal back pain associated with pregnancy, an intravenous antibiotic that could not only destroy her kidneys but harm her baby as well. I felt saddened and defeated in the face of cases like this.

Medical training has since become somewhat more standardized through Mongolia's two medical universities. Nevertheless, these medical schools take their students straight out of ninth grade. After a six-year program with no residency training, they turn out full-fledged doctors, age twenty-one. The most these doctors will ever know is whatever their best professor taught them during their six years. On that they will base their medical practice. The concept of continuing medical education, so taken for granted here, does not exist in Mongolia.

In the years since 1997, we have begun setting up seminars in different places each year, usually near one of the two medical schools. Interpreters from these universities offer their services. The first year, forty Mongolian doctors came to our seminars. Last year, the number reached fifty. We have received good feedback. I believe that this work, done over many years, will have a lasting effect.

Ideally, I would like to spend a week with just one doctor, demonstrating new techniques or refreshing his or her memory. Even such basics as what a physical exam consists of, how it's done, and how you form a diagnosis need to be taught to doctors who never learned them.

Two years ago, I had such a chance. The Good Neighbor Society hired Dr. Saranbat, a graduate of the Mongolian system, to teach health education to rural people. She had the typical round face, ruddy cheeks, and short black hair of her area and wore Western garb under her white lab coat. This good doctor carried a stethoscope put together from the remains of other defunct instruments, as individual pieces were replaced with spare parts when they wore out. I found her mild mannered and dedicated.

Dr. Saranbat had practiced for two years, yet she had no patient interview technique. We started by discussing what questions we should ask (of a man complaining of headaches, for example). By the end of the week, she was conducting the interview and the exam, and making the diagnosis by herself. For me, this reaffirmed the validity of my spending a week with one native doctor. Rather than delivering medical attention, I am empowering local practitioners to do it. If I continue, in fifteen or twenty years my efforts will indeed have a lasting impact.

Ukraine

Orphan's Hope International

A Tale of Two Orphanages

"They have had no job training nor experience shopping, cooking, or handling money. Yet, at the age of sixteen, they are turned out on the street to make room for others."

PAULA WRIGHT

ADMINISTRATIVE ASSISTANT

At fifty-seven, I saw a good many of my peers talking about slowing down, retiring in the not-too-distant future. Jim and I, on the other hand, were looking for something to work into, something that would keep us busy while helping someone else at the same time. Our son Jonathan and daughter-in-law Julie, who had made many trips to Ukraine, piqued our interest with their tales of orphanages there. After all, we love kids, and children—especially orphans—love grandparents.

Orphan's Hope, which Jonathan founded, sends out two teams a year; I have joined three. At the end of the training sessions, held every other week February through June, we sign a promise to bring both God's Word and tangible help, as well as to be respectful of local customs.

181

An orphanage in Ukraine houses not only true orphans, but also children of families in which one parent has died or in which the parents are simply too poor to take care of their offspring. It really resembles a poorhouse for kids. The numbers astounded us. The region of Odessa, for example, boasts eighty-six orphanages of three hundred children each, more than twenty-five thousand youngsters. They even specialize: the eye problem orphanage, the mental health problem orphanage, and so on. The orphanages in which we worked stood in smaller cities, Kotofsk and Izmail. In both cases, when we got there, we didn't know where to stop helping.

The orphanage in the small town of Kotofsk, like most in Ukraine, offers a summer camp. Here we spent all day with the three hundred or so children, except during their rest period after lunch. The camp lay totally isolated, there being no telephone or communication to the outside world. Neither was there any electricity or drinkable water, although cold, nonpotable water ran in the kitchen. The dormitories stood like army barracks with beds from the 1940s, their metal springs covered by a two-inch-thick mattress. On the good side, the Ukrainians are a clean people. The dormitories contained washed bedding and no dirt or bugs.

They did not include a bathroom. Team members used a single outhouse with a hole in the ground, no seat or toilet paper. The children used the public outhouse, a cement structure having eight holes, no seats, no stalls, no privacy, and no septic system.

Each morning, a posted list gave each child his or her chore for the day. Some worked out in the fields, weeding, hoeing, or harvesting their food. Others gathered the dead twigs that had fallen from the trees, binding them together to form brooms with which to sweep the grounds. Still others brought out rugs to hang over lines and beat clean, while others scrubbed the floors. All washed their own bedding and clothing (perhaps two outfits) in the thirty-two sinks that stood outdoors under a roof without walls. Their belongings, we were told, they kept in their pillowcases. Field trips were unknown.

The orphanage director had rigged up a shower—a fifty-gallon tank of water heated by the sun and resting above a building separated from the public toilets. The building remained locked at all times and was only opened for us at night. We had to hurry, one at a time, twenty of us, while the keeper of the key stood outside waiting to lock up again.

The children only showered once every two weeks. When I was a child in the 1940s and '50s, we bathed and washed our hair once a week. Now we do it every day, but not all countries have such luxury. In truth, the children needed it more often, as they walked and worked in the fields and the dirt, and the younger ones spilled food on themselves. When my son and his wife arrived with a large donation of clothing, they got permission for the children to get a shower before putting on their new clothes. My husband, for his part, got a large hotel's donation of soap and shampoo, which he divided among the eager children.

The ages run from six to sixteen. The children are smaller than their counterparts in the States, due, I believe, in large part to their not getting enough protein and milk. Regarding food in general, they need so much more than what they get. Their daily diet consists of cabbage, potatoes, cucumbers, and tomatoes that they grow themselves. Every morning at 7:00, those whose names are posted for this duty go out to the fields with shovels and hoes, singing like Snow White's seven dwarfs, returning at 9:00 for breakfast. The soil is rich and black and offers good potatoes. But potatoes, no matter how good, do not form a healthy daily diet when complemented only by a few other vegetables.

Occasionally, people from Kotofsk would bring in donations of bread. The cooks for the orphanage also baked bread, although they only seemed to do it once a week, which meant the bread gradually became harder and more rationed as the days went by. Our daughter-in-law had arranged beforehand for a taxi driver from Kotofsk to come out a couple times a week to take her to the town market to buy meat and other staples. He would show up when he wanted, and she would drop whatever she was doing to get the chance to buy fruit, meat, cheese, and bread for the children.

Although they are undernourished, the children have never known—nor do they expect—anything else. We, on the other hand, brought peanut butter and jelly, breakfast bars, and other small snacks, eating them privately so as not to give the impolite impression that we were not getting enough to eat, which was the plain truth.

It remains easy to generalize about countries, peoples, and institutions, yet anywhere and everywhere, one individual can make a difference. I never saw any of the Kotofsk orphans receive affection from teachers or the director, whereas the director of the orphanage in Izmail loved the children and was constantly hugging one crying child or another. This marvelous woman—Dina by name—has spent thirty-seven years as director. Although she is married and has a family, she works from 6:00 in the morning until 10:00 at night for "her" children. They have meat and eat fresh bread every other day. The teachers give 5 percent of their salary back to the orphanage. This money has allowed them to paint the walls and have running water for indoor bathrooms (still no seat or toilet paper). The children have shoes and clean clothes.

One day, Jim asked Dina what, if she had her choice, she would most like to have for the orphanage. She hesitated and reddened a little. Please, Jim insisted, tell me. Well, she said, of the 305 children

in her care, 120 were girls between the ages of twelve and sixteen. They had nothing—not even rags—for when they menstruated, and she didn't know what to do.

Jim went to the local pharmacy in Izmail, a closet-sized business that offered buyers three or four toothbrushes, a couple tubes of toothpaste, a few assorted medicines in limited quantities, and a total of three boxes of Kotex. By the most fortunate of coincidences, the representative for Proctor & Gamble was due to visit the pharmacy that day. Jim waited for him and arranged to buy a supply of sanitary napkins that would last the orphanage for six months.

A nurse works at the Izmail orphanage, and a doctor comes once a month. The Kotofsk orphans have nothing. As an example, one of the girls there had one side of her jaw swollen from an abscessed tooth. For her there was no dentist, no doctor, only a poultice. When I went to Kotofsk, I took medical supplies: bandages, children's aspirin, bacitracin. The team that followed included a doctor.

Last year, when the second team went to Kotofsk, they found only half the children at the summer camp. The rest had remained in town, explained the director. Through our interpreter, who overheard two of the teachers talking, we learned the truth. Due to an outbreak of measles, half of the children were under quarantine, right there under our noses, hidden in their dormitories and not allowed out. The deceit was outrageous. Three of our Ukrainian translators, in their twenties, had never had measles. One of our interpreters was pregnant. Thirty of us had walked right into a camp where 150 sick children were hidden so we wouldn't see them. Our pregnant interpreter left but later lost her baby—not because of measles, a local doctor told her, but I'm sure that she will always wonder.

The atmosphere of deceit and fear pervades much of Ukraine. In 1999, we saw many men outfitted in green with machine guns in the airports. They seemed fewer in 2000, and fewer still in 2001. Yet even those remaining frighten the unaccustomed Western traveler. You don't want to attract their attention, as you don't really know where they might take you or put you. You walk by, eyes averted, trying to look like everybody else.

Many of the items available in the United States can actually be purchased in Ukraine. Jim found and bought exercise equipment for the Izmail orphanage. I have seen cell phones and BMWs. In contrast to the United States, however, only a very limited proportion of the population can afford them.

The majority of Ukrainians live in near poverty. A man who works in a tire production plant, for example, may get his pay in tires. To get money, he has to sit out on the highway after work to try to sell the tires. Likewise, a worker in a sugar factory receives sacks of sugar. He and other workers line up along the highway to see who will buy sugar. With several men selling, the man who offers the lowest price will make the sale, although it may be a pauper's pay that he gets.

The government is also poor, or deceitful, or perhaps both. The children don't always get all that their government theoretically sends. If the government is low on money, the orphanage staff does not get paid. In reality, many of these workers are nearly as destitute as their charges. Our hope for the future includes helping not only the orphans, but the teachers and staff as well.

A local farmer helps the children of Kotofsk as they till their fields. He has experience and teaches them about planting. My husband approached him one day. What would he do, he asked, if he could get him a tractor and a disk? If it really got here, the man answered, he would have one season to plant and harvest and become more successful. Then, when the state inspectors came through, they would take it away. He went on to explain, in answer to Jim's puzzled expression, that the tractor would enable him to become self-sufficient, and the government didn't want that. How unjust such governmental control appears in our country, which applauds self-sufficiency and individuality.

We get around the government in any way we can. Eventually we plan to work through Ukrainian nationals who will not only inform us of the items likeliest to get through, but will see to it that they end up with the orphans for whom they are destined. There is always the fear that items sent will be opened on the docks and sold on the black market. Nevertheless, Dina has asked us to send tangibles rather than money. She has to prove to the satisfaction of government inspectors how she has come by every single penny of currency that she has.

Instead of money, we sent a large shipment of wallpaper, blankets, boots, and warm clothing.

The orphanages frequently have no heat, even in the winter. Whether because there isn't enough, or just out of meanness, I don't know, but the powers that be decide if and when a sector of the city needs or doesn't need heat, and turn it off accordingly. The people who live there are not the ones who control it. When Julie accompanied a team last March, she could see her breath even inside the buildings.

In December, an ice storm passed through both Kotofsk and Izmail. Back in the States, we worried about the children. Did they have heat? Had our warm clothes arrived? People here complain about the electricity going out for a few hours so they can't watch television. These vulnerable children, on the other hand, face the real danger of frostbite. In this case, we learned, everything had arrived, both for the orphans of Kotofsk and those of Izmail.

Dina's first concern has always been the children. She tries to make them into well-behaved youngsters and good citizens. The state will provide higher education to those who wish to go on. Nevertheless, a lonely child needs constant reinforcement that he or she can do this. Three of the teachers on Dina's staff are themselves former orphans. One stated that she had become what she is thanks to Dina—because she always knew that she loved her and wanted the best for her. What a director! Yet, she must be my age. How much longer can she work? What will become of these children then?

The orphans, as I mentioned earlier, range in age from six to sixteen. In all their years at the orphanage, they had have no job training nor experience shopping, cooking, or handling money. Yet, when they finish the equivalent of high school at age sixteen or seventeen, they are turned out on the street to make room for others. The route for many of them leads to the army, alcoholism, or prostitution.

Jonathan has approached the church in Izmail about the idea of foster care for these children, a sort of halfway house to life in the real world. For each child, he would need to raise funds equivalent to $30 a month to pay families—poor themselves—to take on an additional mouth to feed. Orphan's Hope works toward this goal.

We Americans have so much. We need to get out there and share. Otherwise we just look inward. We forget that we need to help. Our help does leave its mark. One of the youngest children at the Izmail orphanage remembered me when I returned after a year's absence.

"I remember the song you taught me," she said through the interpreter as she held my hand.

"Can you sing it to me?" I asked.

My eyes filled with tears as she sang a fair rendition of "Jesus Loves Me."

Nicaragua

Global Ministries, Interfaith Service to Latin America

A Degree of Control

"She was thirty-eight.
She had had thirteen pregnancies and had eleven living children."

ELIZABETH MULLIN

RETIRED NURSE

I think I'm hooked. I've traveled to Latin America for the past five years, going twice in 2001 and planning to go twice in 2002. Some people have it even worse. My husband goes three times a year.

We began by going with a leader from our church under the auspices of Global Ministries, an arm of the Methodist Church. Starting in Tegucigalpa and Managua, we gradually narrowed our focus to Jalapa, Nicaragua. A couple years earlier, a Methodist missionary had introduced some people from Rochester, Minnesota, to this town located in the northern highlands near the Honduran border. The thirty thousand or so inhabitants were those who had survived the region's long, drawn-out Sandinista-Contra battles.

Eventually, we formed our own group, Interfaith Service to Latin America (ISLA), and continue to serve in Jalapa. Workers come from our church, a church in Rochester, and as far away as Montana and

Indiana, as word of mouth travels. Half to two-thirds of our members are repeaters. They represent many religious faiths, including Jewish, Muslim, and Christian as well as agnosticism.

A trip lasts about twelve days. Our flight arrives in Managua at night. Early the next morning, we board the bus with all our equipment for the six- or seven-hour journey to Jalapa. In 1999, after Hurricane Mitch, the ride took ten hours, as the bridges over six or eight of the rivers we had to cross had been destroyed. We forded each one, our fingers crossed that we wouldn't get stuck in the middle.

We stay in a Pepto-Bismol-pink motel with the imaginative name of Hotelito #1. Here we share double or triple rooms, usually with the convenience of electricity—and cold running water when the electricity is working. The cook, Mama Chunga, prepares traditional foods with the proper hygiene, bottled water, and refrigeration. Three times a day, she makes rice and beans and beans and rice with subtle variations, along with a few American dishes, delicious rice puddings, and *pastel de tres leches,* a wonderful sweet cake made with three kinds of milk.

All of us work out of the Jalapa hospital, a turquoise and brown single-story structure with a flat, corrugated tin roof. The maintenance portion of the team paints, fixes, and installs. We bring everything, including tools, as the hospital itself has nothing. (A guard went to Robert, my husband, to ask for a hammer, as the hospital had none.) One year when we arrived, we found eleven of the twelve hospital toilets plugged. The hospital had no shelving, so our team installed shelves. They rewired the hospital to allow for proper functioning of the fluorescent lights, motors, and computers.

The medical portion of the team enlists nurses and doctors of different specialties. In 1999, I worked on tubal ligations. The clinic offered running water (not drinkable) and an operating room with open, screenless windows through which insects flew and little boys peered. Previous groups had even brought their own light and operating table.

Our work over many trips has impressed the Nicaraguan government to the extent that they have given the hospital a grant enabling the installation of washable tile on the floor and halfway up the operating room walls. New rules no longer allow street clothes in the room. The windows have been bricked in and air conditioning installed.

Even though the society is Roman Catholic, women line up in droves to have a tubal ligation, many carrying their latest baby. The numbers have dropped off somewhat in the last few trips. I do not know whether this is due to a new priest, who may be speaking against this practice, or whether we have treated so many women in Jalapa that the need has gone down. Nevertheless, the numbers still amaze me. Announcements go out over the radio, and the service is free. As for other forms of birth control, I know that the hospital gives free birth control pills to some women, but I do not know the requirements for receiving them. Many of the pills they give out are the ones we have donated.

One woman, wearing the typical, tight Nicaraguan miniskirt and a bright pink blouse, came in literally begging to have her tubes tied. She was thirty-eight. She had had thirteen pregnancies and had eleven living children. On examining her, we discovered an umbilical hernia, which precluded our laparoscopic procedure. We explained that we could offer a vasectomy for her husband instead. She replied, dejectedly, that he wouldn't come. The interpreter talked at length to the husband, who did agree to come the next day. As the next morning waned, he didn't show, but the woman returned, desperate. Unable to go in through her navel, we would have to make a longer and lower cut

over the ovaries, we explained. We would have to go through more tissue, and we had no general anesthesia. She didn't care. With nothing but Valium and local anesthesia, we performed the operation. She must have been in pain, yet she was smiling. My Spanish is poor, but I understood the much repeated *"Gracias, gracias, gracias."*

Although vasectomies are simple, and we offer the incentive (attractive to many) of a big shot of whiskey, we have done no more than twenty in the five years I have made these trips. We fight an uphill battle in a culture that remains *machista*. The alternative—tubal ligation—offers women a degree of control over their lives. We follow an elaborate procedure for consent, assuring that the woman understands that she will have no more children.

The prevalent machismo is but one of the cultural differences between the United States and Nicaragua. I remember overhearing the shocked voices of two gynecologists dismayed by the sight of a woman obviously in the last stages of ovarian or endometrial cancer. Having been a cancer nurse myself, I recognized the elephant-sized legs, swollen belly, inability to eat, and general weakness. She probably had a few weeks left at most. The shock of my fellow doctors rested not so much in the state of the woman (she had no pain medication, of course) as in the fact that neither she nor her family had a clue as to what was wrong with her. She came hoping for a cure. No local doctor had told her the truth.

One faces an ethical question when working in a society in which custom and culture dictate that the truth not be told if it is unpleasant. American ethics, on the other hand, declares that a patient has the right to know. Our doctors trusted their instincts, telling both the patient and her family that there was little they could do. In this case, both were grateful, particularly her daughters, who realized their limited opportunity to spend quality time with their mother. The family received pastoral counseling from our leader, who now makes regular financial contributions toward the education of two of these girls.

The one unfortunate case I personally dealt with concerned a young woman who had two children and came in for a tubal ligation. The interpreter went through the explanation necessary for consent. She would have no more children. Yes, she understood. As I led her into the operating room, the woman erupted with a spate of rapid Spanish beyond my comprehension. The surgery went on. After the operation, I discovered through an interpreter that the woman's reason for having her tubes tied rested not on the fact that she wanted no more children, but rather that only one breast produced milk. With no money to buy milk, she felt she could not afford to have a child she could not properly sustain. We had not been aware of her reasoning or her problem, and therefore had made no attempt to solve it in some other way. This case continues to bother me.

While I spent my days preparing women for tubal ligations, my husband Robert ("Roberto" in Jalapa) had work of his own. A retired professor of horticulture from the University of Minnesota, he saw the long waiting lines in the dreary halls and the cheerless outer court-yards of the hospital. Something should be done to make the ambiance more pleasant for the patients, he decided.

He began, on our first trip, by planting cheerful gardens outside. That year, they were destroyed by hungry cows. His next attempt fell to the insects and the careless feet of patients. Undaunted, he fenced off a series of courtyards, bought plants from a local nursery, and hired boys off the street to dig, carry, and plant. Most of these "street children" actually have a home and may or may not go to school, yet they spend most of their waking hours shining shoes or performing other menial tasks for a living. They rejoiced at the chance to earn better than their normal pay to make the hospital more attractive. The choice in outdoor plants includes most of those sold here as indoor ornamentals. Both outer and inner courtyards of the hospital now cheer patients with hibiscus, crotons, coleus, fiddle-leaf figs, and other tropical plants, as well as vinca, impatiens, cosmos, morning glory, and sunflowers.

He has also bought a hundred fruit trees to be planted and cared for by local workers. Eventually, this will provide fruit to amplify both hospital workers' and patients' limited diet of rice and beans.

Between the two of us, we brighten the lives of the people in Jalapa, from installing wiring for light bulbs, to planting attractive surroundings, to offering women a better future for themselves and their children. Like other members of the team, we show them that somebody else in the world cares about them. We show them respect. This, I think, remains our greatest contribution. In return, the Jalapeños (yes, that really is what they call themselves) offer us friendship and an unforgettable sense of satisfaction.

COSTA RICA

Volunteer Optometric Service for Humanity

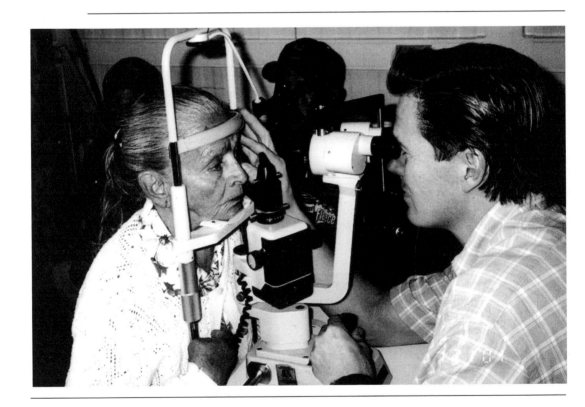

Walking the Thin Line

"You can't go to a place and change it in five days."

MARSHALL EVERSON
OPHTHALMOLOGIST
AND
LENORE EVERSON
RADIOLOGIST

Ten thousand pairs of glasses comprised typical cargo for the Volunteer Optometric Service for Humanity team we took to Costa Rica. This international organization, composed primarily of optometrists, distributes the glasses collected by Lions Clubs across the United States. Volunteers categorize the glasses and file them in boxes by prescription. Two or three times a year, VOSH takes them on a mission to a country where local Lions members, identified by their yellow vests, assist with organization and crowd control. People sit in front of an automated refractor that prints out a prescription for the needed glasses, which are dispensed for free out of the appropriate box. On this trip, we left five thousand glasses for the capital city of San José, taking the other five thousand with us to our base at the nearby city of

Alajuela. In four days, we handed them all out. Our team also offered surgery for cataract removal.

While local Lions traditionally host groups such as ours, a lot of planning and organization goes into any given trip from our end as well. Drug companies have to be contacted for eye-related donations. Syringes, implants, sutures, blades, and operating microscopes must be collected. Furthermore, we research and take into consideration the local conditions, beliefs, and sentiments. If we do not, subsequent groups will pay the price. As an example, another well-intentioned organization worked more or less uninvited in an area of Brazil where local doctors resented the intrusion. As a result, even though our organization intended only to deal with the backlog of ophthalmologic cases that local Brazilian doctors could not handle, we were refused entrance to Brazil—one day before our group was to fly there.

We try not to foster similar situations, because some local people, reacting with normal pride, may resent our help. To prevent this, we try to identify useful contacts beforehand—the mayor or important doctors, for example. Our mutually advantageous association raises the status of these professionals while it assures us of an official welcome. In return for their sponsorship, we make sure that we treat their families and friends. The workday sharing of professional knowledge and after-work socialization with local doctors benefits both sides. Properly laid groundwork raises the likelihood of a receptive climate among the general public as well. The San José newspaper came out with a front-page photograph of one of our surgeries.

In Alajuela, some of the team stayed in people's homes while we and others stayed in the dorm of a technical school. The spartan cement rooms boasted the usual tropical bugs and bats and a bathroom down the hall, conditions mitigated for us Minnesotans by the pleasure of seventy-degree January temperatures. The food, by contrast, was phenomenal. We savored the rice, chicken, fish, and especially fresh fruit, whose exquisite flavor had suffered none of the loss associated with the packed, shipped, and refrigerated counterpart we buy in the United States.

The fact that Costa Rica is not as poor as other lesser-developed countries took us by surprise. (One of us had previously worked in Nicaragua, another in Thailand.) The "Ticos" do not consider themselves Third World residents. A beautiful land, Costa Rica claims no military, boasts a high literacy rate, holds a long tradition of democracy, and offers a population at once friendly and reserved, humble yet self-assured. In this land of geographic contradictions, you can experience fourteen different ecosystems within an area smaller than West Virginia. As for human contradictions, you can eat at a nice restaurant in which a small boy begs to shine your shoes at nine or ten at night. The endless line of people that wait for glasses or hope for a cataract operation runs the gamut from well-dressed and wealthy to terribly poor.

A two-tiered health insurance consists of private insurance and healthcare for the wealthy, and national insurance and healthcare for the rest. Under this system, an ordinary person can wait from three to five years for simple cataract surgery, during which time his or her sight dims to blindness accompanied by a loss of independence. Imperfect and backlogged as it is, the national health system does what it is able in serving those it can.

No one gets a reminder to make an appointment, of course. People receive things on a need-only basis. A bench along a concrete wall forms a typical waiting room. A maternity room may hold thirty pregnant women in a single, large ward. In the decaying, perhaps one-hundred-year-old hospital in which we worked, the radiology equipment consisted of one ultrasound, a thirty- or forty-year-old X-ray

machine, no CAT scanner, and no MRI. Cataract operations were performed with equipment not used in the States for fifteen years.

Dedication of the hospital staff did not seem to suffer under these impediments. In fact, it seemed to make them more creative. In the operating room where the two of us worked as a team (Marshall as surgeon, Lenore as translator and operating nurse), an OR tech named José proved himself an invaluable master of all trades. The hospital owned no laser tip to cauterize blood vessels, so José used a hemostat heated in an open flame. When an earth tremor caused the electricity to go out in the middle of cataract surgery on our operating bed, while an appendectomy took place on the next, José called in everyone who had a flashlight. We waited while he ran an extension cord to another building that still had light. Our hearts beat fast as the darkened minutes ticked by, but there's only so much you can do.

The average age of the hospital's equipment probably stood in the twenty- or thirty-year range. We met a doctor who was trying to buy updated equipment and get American hospitals to donate. We ourselves brought in a ton of equipment and supplies. While they eventually expressed sincere gratefulness, the initial reaction to our donation proved testy, to the tone of "What are you bringing this for?" Costa Ricans have their pride. You have to walk a thin line.

Likewise, while the Costa Rican doctors appreciated the help we gave in reducing their backlog of work, we had to do it their way or risk offense. They determined the patients, leaving us unable to help a local Lion who needed surgery but was not on their list, or the hapless Nicaraguan refugees with whom we would have liked to make contact. (These refugees, similar in status to illegal immigrants in the States, have no access to the health system. Many have waited so long for critical operations that they are past helping.)

The work schedule also followed local dictates. Whereas Marshall had done ten surgeries a day on an earlier mission in Nicaragua, we could manage no more than six in Alajuela. The local staff functioned under a set schedule and time frame. We could not bypass the morning "fruit break," for example. While the fruit proved delicious, we would have preferred to squeeze in another surgery during this time. But we could think of no way to eliminate this customary workday break—a necessity to the Costa Ricans—without creating problems.

The occasional faux pas remained inevitable, it being impossible to switch mental and psychological gears 100 percent to think like another culture. In an open ward, candidates for cataract surgery— buxom women with bodies that told of having carried many children— stood only partially covered by front-opening gowns too small for them. Instinctively, Lenore offered one of the women a second gown for the front. She received as a reward a dirty look from one of the local nurses. "We can't afford to do that," she said, and, of course, she was right. They don't have enough gowns.

You can't go to a place and change it in five days. You just do what you can within the context of respect for local doctors, patients, and conditions.

We'll be doing mission trips for a long time to come. The advantages of working as a couple are in large part personal. We both like learning new things, and this way we share what we do—not only the experiences but the rewards. We earn the satisfaction of having done something good and positive together, something beyond home and children. We've expanded our world. In terms of organization, our partnership will be advantageous on future teams comprised mainly of novices, for we can count on each other's experience.

In the future, we'll take our children—currently eleven, eight, and five—with us. For the moment, we consider them too young for what would probably prove a psychological shock. Even the delivery of church Christmas baskets to local poor people left our son unable to sleep for two nights. But as they grow, we want our children to realize what life is like elsewhere and how lucky they are to live in the United States and Minnesota.

Trips such as this one can't fail to open your eyes, expand your horizons, make you reevaluate yourself, keep you sharp, and force you to face your weaknesses. They further the understanding of another culture and compel you to put things in perspective, both in your medical practice and in your personal life. Prospective volunteers need the desire to help others, the motivation to work hard under less than optimal conditions, and especially the willingness to enter new adventures.

One always wants to do more. We can't forget the sobering incidents in which we had to turn patients away just because we couldn't take any more. Did we make a difference with what we did do? Thirty surgeries and 5,000 glasses didn't make a huge dent in what needs to be done in Costa Rica or the world, but we did change the lives of those 5,030 people. The greatest reward in eye work is giving people back something they've lost. Those grateful glasses owners can once again see long distances or read a book. The recipients of cataract surgery—many of whom were legally blind and had lost their balance and coordination—again have some independence. Furthermore, the techniques we taught the two local doctors will continue to bear fruit in our absence.

The rewards exceed the sacrifices. Costa Ricans do not have the American sense of entitlement. As a result, they prove to be wonderful patients, extremely appreciative. This thankfulness extends through their families, leading to lots of hugs from grateful children, grandchildren, siblings, and others.

The greatest reward lies in using the fundamentals of medicine to help someone, unhindered by complications of red tape, insurance, or lawyers. This back-to-basics practice of medicine is all but lost in the United States and possibly in any developed country. Experiencing it elsewhere renews your sense of why you went into medicine in the first place.

Russia, Philippines, Kenya

Resurrection Life Church, The Love Call

The Language of Love

*"Of the people involved in missions, perhaps 20 percent actually travel.
Then there are those who organize and send the ones who go,
and the many who pray for them."*

HOLLY BRIGGS

REGISTERED NURSE

Russia had just opened its doors, and 1991 proved an exciting time to minister. I went with the evangelical SALTeam Ministries from my church and served as a singer on a worship team. (SALT stands for Sending Appointed Lay Teams.)

Like all baby boomers, I grew up in the 1950s with the fear of Russia. The shock, forty years later, of seeing the conditions under which the people lived has remained with me. The government could not meet even the basic needs of its citizens. We visited hospitals and orphanages, homes for the retarded and disabled. The orphanages proved appalling, with some of the children tied to their beds. Terrible conditions also prevailed in the equivalent of our nursing homes. Outside of institutions, up to three generations lived in one small apartment.

After that memorable trip, I began to help coordinate the medical arm of SALT. Somehow, I felt that God was calling me to go, and I was compelled to help. I filled two forty-foot containers with medical supplies and shipped them overseas, the federal government paying for the shipping. The first container went to our contact in St. Petersburg, a doctor at the former Karl Marx Hospital, now known as St. George's. The other went to two village hospitals. I recruited doctors to go on trips and perform surgeries, shipping medical supplies and equipment—even beds—a couple months ahead of the team so they could make use of them upon arrival.

A high proportion of these donated medical supplies came from Fairview. People who did not know my name but referred to me as "the mission nurse" collected items that were destined to be thrown out from

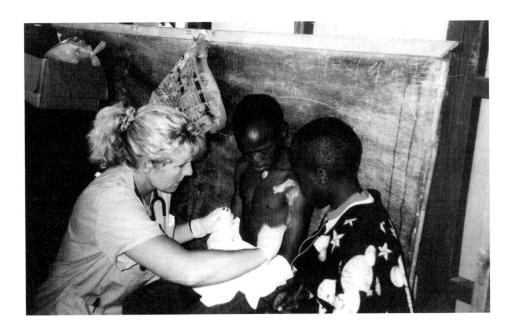

various Fairview hospitals. What we threw away was like gold to the Russians. Each year, we would see the things we had sent the year before. Needles and IV tubing were reused. The people exercised rationing and extreme care, as they never knew when they might get more.

In 1994, a misdirected letter led me to a different part of Russia. Correspondence intended for a doctor with a similar name arrived at the office of a man named Levitov, a Russian doctor living in Minnesota. The letter begged for donations for Russia. Dr. Levitov got in touch with me, telling me about Tuva, the Russian republic from which he came. He proved an invaluable resource, as he knew people in the country who could facilitate our visit.

Halfway across the world, two days by plane from Minnesota, Tuva lies in Siberia, north of Mongolia. Enclosed by mountains, the surrounding area had served as a point of detention for some of Stalin's exiles. The old prisons that we could see from the air hardly seemed necessary. The area was so remote that there was nowhere to go, even if one were not enclosed within walls.

The indigenous people are descended from Genghis Khan. They remain nomadic sheepherders, sheltering in mobile tents known as yurts and living off the land much as their ancestors did. They know no refrigeration and cook their food over an open fire in the middle of the tent. Once in a while they come into Kyzyl, the capital of Tuva. Acrimony and hard feelings remain between the ethnic Tuvans and the Russians. In the days of Stalin, many Russians—like it or not— were relocated to the area, where they received positions of leadership. To this day, many officials are Russian rather than Tuvan.

The Fairview Foundation helped to buy an instrument necessary to perform microsurgery on ears, and our team brought along an otolaryngologist to teach the local Tuvan doctor how to perform the surgery. The doctor could hardly find the words to express his gratitude.

He had read about this surgery in a magazine but had never dreamed that one day he would be able to offer it to his patients. The first patient to have microscopic ear surgery was the hospital administrator, who had been deaf for some time. The operation proved a success.

When we left, we tied a ribbon on a tree in the center of the city to guarantee our eventual return, as dictated by Tuvan custom.

By 1997, SALTeam Ministries had ceased to exist, and I started my own medical mission, The Love Call. We traveled to the main island of Luzón in the Philippines, specifically to the city of Baguio. On this pioneer trip, we went as a small group with the idea of researching conditions in order to return later with a larger group.

In this area, hospitals lie far apart. Hills and valleys make for rugged terrain; floods frequently cover the roads. A man, having traveled by foot for two days over the mountains, staggered into the hospital carrying his wife on his shoulders. Postpartum hemorrhaging had left her too weak to walk. We had no lab to check her hemoglobin and no Pitocin to stop the bleeding. She would die within a day or two, the doctor informed me. My heart sank as I looked at the woman's husband. Since then, I have never traveled without a bottle of Pitocin. I still remember her face.

Months later, accompanied by a medical team, I took an all-day ride over the mountains to Kabayan, where the mayor and the entire village turned out to greet us at the clinic. They wore their native costumes and performed traditional dances. The Kabayan hospital, under construction, was staffed solely by a five-foot, seventy-five-pound female doctor who lived in the building and worked seven days a week.

Our first morning at the clinic, we saw the entire hillside covered with people wanting to be seen. We worked from dawn till dusk, offering medical, optical, and dental services. We had brought our own Novocain, there being none available locally, and did five hundred extractions. In that single day, we saw thirteen hundred people.

Less than two years later, I took a medical team to Kenya, where we stayed in Nairobi but traveled two or three hours each day to work in more needy areas. Our travels took us into Masai land in the heart of the Serengeti. The skin conditions in the boys' orphanage proved shocking; between scabies and various fungal conditions, I had never seen children so infected. These children contract scabies from dirt, which they dig with their hands and eat because they are so hungry. A microscopic mite enters through cracks in the skin, causing sores over the entire body. The scabies lotion, put on the skin after a bath and left to dry, costs only a few dollars in the States, yet serves dozens of children. Until we came, these children had no treatment and no alternative to living with their miserable sores.

Malaria runs rampant as well. Near Lake Victoria in Kisumu, we saw a three-month-old baby in Nyanza General, the area's main hospital. Her labored breathing indicated a losing fight with this mosquito-borne disease. The overcrowded hospital lacked even basic medicines and had nothing for one so little. We heard the next morning that she had died. I remember thinking how short life can be if you live in a place like this. I have gained such appreciation for how blessed we are in America.

I am committed to going to India, among other places, with a future Fairview grant. My concern for people in developing countries makes me want to serve because not everyone can. Of the people involved in missions, perhaps 20 percent actually travel. Then there are those who organize and send the ones who go, and the many who pray for them. Realistically, I have to work for my living; otherwise, I would involve myself in this full time.

Many times I have come to tears at the enormity of the task. I have seen five hundred people waiting for medical care in a single church and have realized that they are only a tiny portion of all those in need. The hardest thing, when the team reaches the point of exhaustion, is to close the gate on those still outside and say, "No more." I have cried for hours for those unseen and unhelped patients. Yet, if I can help one person or save a single life with an antibiotic, I feel overwhelmingly rewarded.

I am at home in these countries, even though conditions, temperature, skin color, language, and food prove different. I like to think that I travel under God's protection, and that's why I feel at home. Whether in Russia, the Philippines, or Africa, I feel as if I speak their tongue. The commitment to heal needs no translation. The language of love provides common ground.

GUATEMALA

HELPS International

Agenda for Repair:
Equipment and People

"The United States is America.
Guatemala is America.
God bless America."

JAMES HENNESSY
MAINTENANCE MANAGER

In Minnesota, I work as a maintenance manager for Fairview Northland Regional Health Care, a semirural hospital with forty beds and five clinics. My efforts keep the medical and mechanical equipment up and running. In Guatemala, I do much the same thing under more challenging circumstances. The equipment there is vintage 1980s, a combination of Fairview and private donations to HELPS. We store the anesthetic and suction machines, sterilizers, generators, and other equipment in a warehouse in Guatemala City, where each successive HELPS team can access them.

HELPS grew from the combined efforts of a Dallas investment banker and a Wycliffe Bible Translators missionary who went to

Guatemala in the late 1970s to translate the Bible into one of the country's twenty-one Mayan languages. A nondenominational and nonprofit Christian organization, HELPS sends eight medical teams (seventy to ninety people each, including local volunteers) and twelve smaller construction teams yearly to work in the neediest areas of the country. I have heard that Continental Airlines classifies HELPS as the largest medical mover in Central America.

Our team consisted of a plastic surgeon, an obstetric-gynecologist, an ear-nose-throat specialist, a general surgeon, family practitioners, assistants, and dentists. We saw a lot of cancers that in our country would have been detected much earlier, as well as gallbladder problems, hernias, chain-saw injuries, and the inevitable burns caused by children falling into cooking fires.

In the mid-1980s, the president of Guatemala ordered the building of a dozen or so small hospitals in the Guatemalan highlands. These were built by American contractors with American equipment and systems, and are known as *centros de salud* (health centers). In reality, many function as little more that first-aid centers, as the government doesn't have enough qualified people to staff them. These centers, however, serve as excellent bases for us, as we can leave part of our team there while we send others into outlying villages.

We bring in our own materials and equipment. Each member flies down with a team bag of medical supplies in addition to his or her own personal bag. Besides the team bag, I also carry my tools, glues, oils, and tapes, splitting them up between the checked and the carry-on luggage in case one is lost.

The hospitals serve not only as work areas but also as sleeping quarters. I have slept in X-ray film rooms on a folding cot in the warmth of my sleeping bag. The temperature varies depending on what part of Guatemala we visit. The medical teams usually go to the highlands during the first four months of the year, when day temperatures reach the eighties but nights dip into the sixties and fifties. In Joyabaj, where the hospital air conditioning is shot because of the variances in electrical output, the outside temperatures reach eighty-five or ninety while doctors sweat in an eighty-degree operating room. In the hot rain forest of Playa Grande we stifle in the humidity, while we shiver in the cold rain forest of San Cristóbal. In the unheated hospitals, we close the windows to keep out the night cold; the steam boiler serves only the hot water heater and sterilizer. Nevertheless, no one complains. Any climate thrills us as we leave the Minnesota winter.

We bring our own cooks, who use the hospital kitchen to prepare a combination of local products—including wonderfully sweet pineapples—and food brought from the States. We remind each other to close our mouths while taking a shower and brush our teeth in bottled water. The automatic habit of turning on the faucet dies hard.

Guatemala has twice as many people as Minnesota in a geographic area only half the size. Yet, in this small area, there remain regions so remote that Spanish is still unspoken by some of the people, who converse only in their Mayan tongue.

Much of this remoteness and isolation can be accredited to the mountainous terrain and the poor condition of limited roads. I have bounced up and down for hours in a chicken bus normally filled with sandaled peasants holding unhappy fowl upside down while crossing the Cuchumatanes Mountains. I have jostled over dirt roads so bumpy that only my grip on the seat rails has kept me in place. On one occasion, a team member brought a global positioning system to track our as-the-crow-flies progress. After ten and a half hours of curves and hills, bumps and ruts, we had moved a total of sixty-one miles out of Guatemala City.

The towns are not much better. On streets built for horse traffic, bus drivers have an assistant who jumps down at every corner and directs the overly tight turns. These apprentice drivers will someday move up to be drivers themselves and will eventually know the country roads much as a riverboat captain knows a river.

Despite high-profile crimes in Guatemala, I do not dwell on safety concerns. It is true that after Guatemala's civil war, as after our own, some of both the government and guerrilla fighters became criminals—raiders, robbers, and marauders. Yet the vast majority of people are simple, good people. Against those who are not, we take appropriate safety precautions, such as never traveling at night or taking early morning walks alone. On occasion, the police have escorted us through the highlands.

We found ourselves in Antigua when the terrorist attack took place at New York's World Trade Center. The HELPS coordinator in Guatemala asked the team whether we wanted to move to a secure hotel in Guatemala City, such as the Marriott, whose staff is trained in antiterrorist measures. We declined. Our hotel—like most—already had armed guards stationed out front. Security is ever present in Guatemala. Even trucks delivering bottled water carry guards with guns. Poverty-stricken people use neither checks nor credit cards, and a truck delivering bottled water can accumulate a tempting amount of cash by the end of the day. Armed guards stand duty as well at schools, banks, and the homes of the rich. Nevertheless, if and when I experience doubts about the sanity and safety of these missions, I remind myself that God travels with us as a member of the team.

We didn't learn of the September 11 terrorist attack until twelve hours afterward. Not until two days later did we have a chance to view the footage of two planes crashing into the World Trade Center. As we stood dumbfounded around the television in a small restaurant,

the local people—knowing that we came from the United States—waited in respectful silence. Back in Antigua, the owner of another restaurant came up to say how sorry he was. All the employees, he said, had gotten together to say a prayer.

Natalia García de Cuevas, a dignified Antiguan author of books on local art and history as well as the owner of a candle shop in which I have stopped every trip, expressed her sympathy in broken English. For all the times I had visited her shop, I had never known that she spoke my tongue. She had stopped when she heard news of the attack, she said, and prayed in her shop.

Just as these trips reward us with an intimate glimpse into the lives of others, we, too, become known and befriended. One store window displayed in Spanish the handwritten sign, "The United States is America. Guatemala is America. God bless America." Ambassador

Bushnell put an ad in the major Guatemalan papers thanking the people for their solidarity with us.

The Guatemalans were as shocked by the events of September 11 as we were. They understand atrocities and empathize with their victims because they themselves have been victims. Santa Avelina, one of the villages in which we worked, claims an unenviable distinction as one of the hardest hit during the civil war. The guerrillas moved in and occupied Santa Avelina and various other communities. The army, assuming public sympathy for the antigovernment forces, retook the area amid much slaughtering of innocents. The guerrillas, when they again gained the upper hand, did the same. The people remained caught in the middle. What was once a mass grave behind the school has now become a beautiful flower garden tended by the widows of the town.

HELPS construction teams built houses for these widows, whose homes and families had been destroyed. They gave them concrete floors as opposed to the normal dirt, which turned to mud during the rainy season. HELPS is also building them outdoor toilets and laundries, as well as stoves made of concrete and cement. These stoves use only a third of the wood of an open fire, an important advantage in a country where increased deforestation has led to fatal landslides. The new stoves also evacuate the smoke out of the house. (Many of the raspy coughs and red eyes we treated resulted from constant exposure to the smoke of cooking fires in unventilated houses.) Best of all, these stoves do not pose the danger to children of the traditional open fires.

Yet even this small degree of modernization has to follow the dictates of local custom. If an Ixil woman of childbearing age cooks with a closed lid, local wisdom says, her child will be stillborn. So our teams designed an outdoor stove, half of a metal barrel with a clay firebox and no top, for use by the women. The regular indoor stoves consisted of a concrete firebox with an iron plate over the top and a pipe to vent the smoke.

Here in Minnesota, there was a time when I would have become frustrated if my garage door opener or other expected convenience did not work. These things no longer bother me.

In the Guatemalan highlands, the lighting generally consists of a single low-watt bulb hanging by its cord from the ceiling. The power might go out anytime. Many times the operating room goes dark in the middle of a surgery. The unpredictable voltage can drop from 125 to 70, necessitating a generator for anything better. The luxury of hot showers is afforded only by the hospital boiler, its steam put to use heating shower water. Outside of the hospital, we depend on our propane water heater. American doctors are not used to this, but Guatemalans accept it as a part of everyday life.

I installed two water tanks in Santa Avelina to store the water from a waterfall above the village. I put in pumps to give water to the school, located on high ground and left waterless by the running faucets of houses on lower ground. I fixed broken machines and rewired nonfunctioning parts.

In the United States, we are losing the art of fixing things. We prefer to dispose of broken items and get new ones. In Guatemala, the cost of labor remains low while the cost of new items lies out of reach. Of necessity, things get fixed. I have learned how to repair anything and get it working again—adequately, if not perfectly.

We fix not only equipment, but people. This year, we operated on a twenty-eight-year-old woman with a cleft lip. Refusing a photo, she sat in the waiting room with her hand covering her mouth, her eyes beaming because she was going to have surgery. We fixed more than just her lip. Finally looking like other girls, she now had the chance to get married. In some sectors, people still believe that a mother must have done something bad to have borne a child like this. We left her free of stigma. We also operated on a woman who had spent her entire seventy-nine years with a cleft lip.

I have seen untreated burns so bad that the scar tissue bends the arm or leg to the point of uselessness. We alleviate the problem with skin grafts at the elbow or the knee. As the grafts can take several hours, we do them in the evenings, working into the night.

One Saturday morning in Joyabaj, a panicked mother ran through the gate with a nonbreathing child in her arms. Team members carried the little girl into the operating room where other members were busy packing up. Two anesthesiologists and two emergency room physicians began resuscitation techniques while someone else called the fire department, which also provides the ambulance service. On the two-hour trip to the regional hospital, two paramedics from the team continued life support, and the child survived. One of the players in this little drama was a burned-out paramedic questioning his future in this very intense line of work. Helping to save this child's life renewed his faltering conviction that he had found his calling.

Also in Joyabaj, an old man arrived to take his wife home after surgery. Their home lay four miles over the hills via one of the old Mayan foot trails packed hard by countless indigenous feet over hundreds of years. As the woman could not make that kind of a trek after surgery, the staff tied a wooden chair to the husband's back, then secured the wife in the chair. Bent over from the weight, the old man turned to the team members and thanked them.

Somehow, the more we help others, the more we find ourselves rewarded and enthused by our work. Skilled professionals do what they entered the medical field to do. Surgeons perform surgery for hours. Doctors and nurses spend their time healing, not writing medical records or filling out insurance forms. They deal only with repairing physical and emotional health.

In Playa Grande in the northern part of the country, refugees are returning in the aftermath of the civil war. Some seventy-five thousand people in this jungle area have no healthcare. On my next trip, I will remain an extra week to help a team coming in from Oregon as they minister to their health needs.

We share so little with others, yet that little makes so much difference. The best thank-you I have ever received I got in Guatemala from an elderly man who insisted on shaking everyone's hand. "I can't give you anything," he lamented, "but God will bless you for what you've done for us."

ZIMBABWE

Volunteers in Medical Missions

Part of My Life

*"They have no understanding of what modern medicine can do for them.
It's like they're living in another century."*

BEV DOEDEN

RETIRED NURSE

Praise the Lord! We slept in until 7:00 A.M.

So begins my diary entry for June 7, 2001. On that day, I found myself working in Zimbabwe, the latest of four countries to which I had traveled with Volunteers in Medical Missions.

Venezuela and India held in common the immense crush of people in a small area. India in particular demonstrated a noise level of horn and human and animal sounds unequaled by any din in my experience before or since. The Ukrainian people stood apart as less ebullient than the others. I had seen them stand somberly in line for hours with hardly a word, their reticence to show any emotion ingrained, I supposed, by years of Communist domination. By contrast, the people of Venezuela, India, and Zimbabwe proved happy and demonstrative. I considered Zimbabwe the most colorful of the countries in its natural beauty, although similar to the other three in the poverty of the people and their gratitude for anything we could do for them.

I had come to Zimbabwe via a circuitous route. Years earlier, my uncle, a pastor in Indonesia, had found a boy sleeping in the church closet. It became a family project to educate this young man, who eventually became a doctor, and others like him. When my uncle died and I lost my contact with Indonesia, I looked for other avenues to help the less fortunate of the world. Through the invitation of a friend, I discovered Volunteers in Medical Missions.

On this particular morning, I awoke with twenty-four other volunteers in the lodge of the Hwange National Park in Zimbabwe. Our group was large, so we divided daily into four teams and headed through the reserve toward different areas to hold clinics. Of necessity, we got a free safari tour on the way to and from our work each day, as the uncrowded preserve offered us glimpses of elephants, lions, and other animals. At another time, we might have encountered more tourists, but the instability of the country had effectively discouraged most visitors, leaving the wide spaces, tall grasses, and hidden animals to us. As landless native squatters took over more and more of white families' farmland, the farm owners tried to liquidate what they could and leave before possible violence overtook them. The abandonment of once productive farms led, of course, to food shortages. The decline in tourism, combined with the internal upheaval, caused a general economic decline affecting—as always—the poor most of all.

I noted in my diary:

My prayer for these people is that they might get a government that is honest and can share some of the wealth with these poor, struggling people. . . . The Minister of Health has fled to Malaysia—we assume to avoid a deadly "auto accident" or the fatal "malaria" that has befallen several other government officials. I know God is watching over us.

Knowing that God is watching over us has kept me from feeling frightened even when the situation warrants it. My greatest fear—as yet unrealized on any of my trips—concerns snakes. Despite the terrain we traverse, I have never seen one. The elephant that appeared suddenly out of the brush a few feet from our jeep did cause me a few anxious moments. The political situation in Zimbabwe remains a serious consideration, too. However, the people I have met and worked with on this and other VIMM teams have had so much to offer and have been so wonderful that I have found myself unable to be anything but happy in their company.

The people of Zimbabwe needed us. Some twenty years ago, their government had built the clinics in which we worked. Their white-stuccoed walls contain an exam room, a waiting room, a minimal kitchen, running water (via pump), a toilet, and electricity. The phones, unfortunately, are useless, as the government has no money to pay the bills. At one time, these clinics were staffed by traveling dentists and doctors who would treat the local population and live in the clinic until they moved on to the next one. Now, the government can no longer pay them. None of the people we saw had had access to a doctor for months. The clinics stood empty, signs of a country in crisis.

The people are desperately poor, my diary continues, *and grateful for everything we give them. Things have to be passed out secretly or it will create a crowd in seconds.*

We examined and treated over six thousand people in Zimbabwe, a record for VIMM on a single trip. Malaria runs rampant, and probably half the population has AIDS. Statistics give the figure as 40 percent, but that is low. Surprisingly, no one tells these people what they have. Death certificates list the cause of death as TB or malaria. AIDS in Zimbabwe remains a dirty secret no one wants to talk about.

We saw many ten- and twelve-year-old girls with the disease, a result of the prevalent belief that if a man has intercourse with a child, he will be cured of AIDS. Among uneducated people, it's hard to overcome such devastating folk beliefs. I passed out condoms, threatening the men that they would die if they didn't use them.

Even the incidence of malaria could be cut down with a higher level of education. The medicine is available, but people fail to take the whole course because of the bitter taste. They have no understanding of what modern medicine can do for them. It's like they're living in another century. Education remains so vital. I wonder at the people who just pass out Bibles. First you have to teach these people how to read.

Things rarely happen as planned in underdeveloped countries. On our first day, partway through the two- to three-hour drive from the airport to our lodging, the truck in which I was riding—the last in the caravan—had to stop to put air in one of the tires. A couple miles up the road, the tire blew out altogether. The only spare, of course, was on one of the trucks that had disappeared from sight while we were filling the tire with air. After a considerable wait, another vehicle came along. Our driver, without any ado, disappeared into this vehicle and rode off, leaving seven of us stranded alone on a dirt road in ever-darkening gloom in the middle of nowhere.

After a while, I broke out the two little bottles of wine I had taken off the airplane, and for lack of any other option, we celebrated our predicament together. Slowly, on the air of the clear moonlit night, we began to distinguish first one voice, then another, then still others off in the woods. In the distance, we could see what looked like campfires. The voices came closer, and one of our members wandered off to talk to the approaching strangers. One by one we followed, meeting many of the thirty-five people—all relatives, as families remain close in Zimbabwe—who lived there. Some of the children spoke English, so we could communicate using something more than gestures. We promised them clothes, vitamins, and goodies when we passed their way again, mentally marking a large tree under which we would leave them. Finally, someone returned for us, taking us to the hotel for supper, a cold shower, and a very short night. Our driver never reappeared.

But the transportation adventure didn't end there. Days later, on our way back to the airport, our driver noted that the truck didn't sound right. We suggested that it might not be such a good idea to continue driving at seventy-five to eighty miles an hour over a rutty road in a vehicle that was literally falling apart. Too late. A few minutes later, the differential broke. Crowding ourselves into one of the other trucks, we rode like sardines, some in back and half a dozen of us in front. We managed to find the tree and leave gifts for the people who once again appeared out of the woods, elated to have us fulfill our promise. Further on, one of the women wanted to take a photograph of an "elephant crossing" sign. We stopped too fast for the luggage truck closely tailing us. CRASH! What else could go wrong? No one, fortunately, was hurt, but the luggage truck now had more problems than poor brakes. It proved inoperable, so we continued on to the hotel and sent the hotel bus back for the luggage. Never a dull moment!

Some memories I will carry with me for years. One kind, native woman let me see her home—three round clay huts with thatched roofs, a hole for a door, and no windows. One hut functioned as a kitchen, another as her and her husband's sleeping quarters, the third as the children's bedroom. None had any furniture, as the family sat on goatskins. I also remember the sweet and uncomplaining woman in the old folks' home, suffering from a breast cancer tumor that affected her whole chest wall. I remember a mother patiently using a syringe to feed a three-month-old baby with AIDS, unaware that it probably had only a few weeks left to live.

Above all, I remember the gratefulness of the people we helped. They may not read and write, but they understand that we care for them. For my part, I have come to appreciate the efforts of individual Americans. We Americans are not accepted in many parts of the world except for our aid, and many ills over which we have no control are blamed on our country. Nevertheless, in the one-to-one situations I find on these trips, we have a chance to show that we are caring and generous individuals.

Medical missions have become part of my life. I am fully committed. Not only will I continue as long as I am physically able, but I hope someday to take my son and grandson with me. I go to help, yet each time I come back wonderfully rewarded by the delightful people I meet around the world. To not continue would be unimaginable.

Venezuela, Kenya

Operation Smile

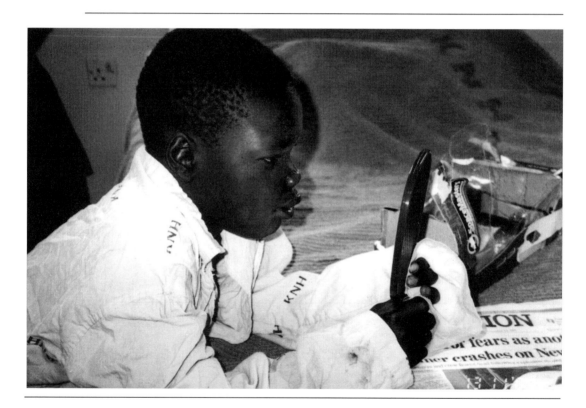

Changing Lives
in Forty-Five Minutes

"Now I'm no longer the monster of my village."

LAUREN BECKSTROM
SURGERY SCHEDULER

Two years ago, as I thought ahead to my third trip with Operation Smile, I faced a shortage of paid time off. I had used most of it by participating in missions the two years previous and on some necessary surgery for myself. What I had left wasn't enough. I stewed for some time about what to do, until a coworker put her hand on my arm one day. "I can't go myself," she said, "but I want to support your effort. I'll give you a week of my vacation."

Her generosity astounded me. It shouldn't have, of course. Fairview has a lot of altruistic people. I took her unexpected offer to my superior, who okayed everything. A few weeks before I was to go, word came from somewhere higher that such a transfer of paid time could be approved only in the case of serious illness, and I didn't qualify. My heart sank.

After some thinking, I sat down and wrote a letter to the Fairview CEO. I drafted and redrafted, boiling my sentiments down to the essentials like the reduction of a sauce on a stove. Not allowing an employee to contribute paid time in support of a charitable medical mission, I wrote, was incongruous with the four values—compassion, dignity, integrity, and service—predicated as part of the Fairview system.

Nine days later, I received a personal letter from the CEO informing me that because of my efforts, the policy regarding donation of paid time would be changed to include medical missions. A short week before the Venezuela trip, word came that I would have my coworker's time. The policy had indeed been changed.

I would have gone—sans pay—even without the donated time, so why did I fight so hard for my employer's support? The CEO understood when he wrote, "Your compassion for those less fortunate exemplifies the ideals that Fairview stands for." I represented Fairview as well as myself.

To explain why I wanted to go at all: I've always been a people person. In high school, I did peer counseling; as an adult, I entered a service vocation that I wanted to extend beyond my immediate community. Further, as a former Spanish major, I looked for opportunities to use the language I had studied and enjoyed. When I was twenty-three, at that time a receptionist at Fairview, an ad in the employee newsletter requested volunteers for Operation Smile, including speakers of Spanish. I signed up for my first trip and have gone every year since.

Unlike many of my companions that first year, I felt prepared for the general conditions one encounters in developing countries. After all, I had studied three and a half months in Guatemala, Colombia, and Ecuador. Nevertheless, having worked in a medical environment at Fairview, I found myself repeatedly shocked by the lack of standards in this area. In Venezuela, I walked down hospital corridors over unswept and unmopped floors, between walls of chipped plaster and peeling paint. Cockroaches crawled in the sinks, and rubber gloves were washed and reused. Hospital elevators malfunctioned as often as not. Thirty to forty women stood in a bedless maternity waiting room, some obviously in labor. At one moment, as the doors to the delivery room swung open, I saw the floor covered with blood. In the hall, one woman hemorrhaged unattended on the floor. We tried to get some help for her. "Oh," came back the unconcerned reply, "we'll be there in a minute." I attributed the low level of medical standards to shortness of both staff and education.

The local government advertised our coming over the radio and in the newspaper for several months prior to our appearance. As Operation Smile deals mainly with cleft lips and palates, people with these or other facial deformities were encouraged to see us. Our team—comprising a dentist, a speech language pathologist, plastic surgeons, pediatricians, anesthesiologists, nurses, and several non-medical volunteers—screened everyone who came. Each patient's chart consisted of the name, address, age, distance traveled to reach the hospital, person he or she came with, and a Polaroid photo. The surgeons rated them on a scale of one to five, one being the most appropriate for and most needing of reparative surgery. After two or three days of screening, we posted a list with the names and the time assigned for each patient to return for a free operation.

We examined everyone, even those who were not candidates for surgery, on the theory that many of them had never seen a doctor in their entire lives. Some cases lay beyond us. We could do nothing, for example, for the little Venezuelan boy whose skull bones were fused, whose eyes popped out of his head like a Halloween mask. In Kenya, a four-year-old girl born without a nose was flown in by missionaries

from Zambia and proved partially treatable. We did some dental work, but we could not construct a nose. In such cases, we tried to direct patients to a better resource. On a few occasions, Operation Smile has brought severe cases to the United States for complicated operations. Most of those that we turned away accepted the refusal once they understood why. A few responded with tears, while a few others showed up in the line two or three times, hoping each time for a different response.

In both countries, we found great support among the local people. They kept order for us in the crowd as people waited to be screened. In Venezuela, the Mare-Mares Golden Rainbow Hotel donated rooms during our stay, as did the Sarova chain in Kenya. The hospitals, of course, lent us the operating rooms.

From Kenya, I particularly remember the case of John, thirteen, a street child deformed by both a cleft lip and cleft palate. When we came to fill out the portion of his chart indicating the responsible adult, we discovered that he had been brought in by Duncan, a cafe owner from a town outside Nairobi, who had been feeding the hungry boy. Duncan had heard of Operation Smile and, although he had no relation or obligation to John, he had driven around the streets until he found the boy, then brought him to us to see if we could help.

After the operation, we gave John a little mirror. He sat for hours, looking first at the Polaroid photo of his face before the operation, then at the new face reflected in the mirror.

For the area, Duncan dressed fairly well, usually in shirt and pants, one day in a suit. His cafe, according to the team member who accompanied him and John one day, was little more than a shack. Yet Duncan generously offered to take John in during his recovery. John spoke little and had never been to school. Team members raised funds to get him into one, as even public schools in Kenya cost money. With this help, John is progressing well and developing a love of books.

I got an e-mail from Duncan recently. "I was very comforted," he wrote, "to see your concern." In Kenya he had told me, "Because of you, John has hope for the future."

This work puts my life in perspective. Even more than before, I appreciate having a loving family, sufficient food, an adequate education. Many people don't have such benefits. I marvel at the work of surgeons who can change a person's life as well as his or her face. A man in Venezuela whose cleft lip we repaired told us after his operation, "Now I'm no longer the monster of my village."

The Kenyans are a compassionate people, but rarely in a hurry to do anything. They get around to their good deeds in their own good time. Our limited time, however, means that we must schedule surgeries to work efficiently without sacrificing patient safety. The surgery to correct a cleft lip takes forty-five minutes. In forty-five minutes, we can change a life. In two weeks, we can change a lot of lives.

A Continuing Call

As stated by a Fairview nurse, there are those who go on missions, those who organize and send the ones who go, and the many who pray for them. Fairview claims active participation in all three groups. As an institution, it not only retains but encourages the sense of mission that was vital to its founders. Through its Medical Missions Committee it offers travel grants, medicine, supplies, and equipment to those willing to form part of a mission team.

Organizations through which Fairview volunteers have channeled their talents to benefit others include:

Archdiocesan AIDS Ministry—Fairview-University Medical Center, Riverside Campus, 2450 Riverside Avenue, Minneapolis, MN 55454; or call (612) 672-4345

Common Hope—http://www.commonhope.org

Curamericas—www.curamericas.org

Global Ministries—http://gbgm-umc.org

Helping Hands— http://nepal.cudenver.edu/helpinghands/helpinghands.html

HELPS International—http://www.helpsintl.org

International Health Service—http://www.ihsofmn.org; or call Cheryl Schrader at (952) 996-0977

Interplast—http://www.interplast.org

The Love Call—The Love Call, c/o Resurrection Life Church, 16397 Glory Lane, Eden Prairie, Minnesota 55344; or e-mail: thelovecall@hotmail.com

Lutheran Health Care/Bangladesh—http://www.lhcb.org

Open Arms of Minnesota—http://www.openarmsmn.org

Operation Smile—http://www.operationsmile.org

Orphan's Hope International—
  http://www.orphanshopeinternational.org

Pro Health International—local contact Shirley Graf (651) 982-7106

Project Haiti—123 Minnesota Avenue South, Aitkin, Minnesota
  56431; or call (218) 927-2634

Resource Exchange International—REI-Vietnam, 1855-C, Austin
  Bluffs, Colorado Springs, Colorado 80918; or call (719) 528-5126

Volunteer Optometric Service for Humanity—http://www.vosh.org

Volunteers in Medical Missions—http://www.vimm.org

Witness for Peace—http://www.witnessforpeace.org

World Servants—http://www.usa.worldservants.org; Minnesota
  office (612) 866-0010

World Vision—http://www.worldvision.org

Youth Adventures—http://www.youthadventures.org

Among others, these Minnesota churches have sent volunteer groups:

Cornerstone Church, St. Cloud

Edinbrook Church, Brooklyn Park

Friendship Church, Prior Lake

Resurrection Life Church, Eden Prairie

Twin Cities Chinese Christian Church, Lauderdale

Wooddale Community Church, Eden Prairie

Individual Fairview volunteers—receptionists, therapists, pharmacists, nurses, and doctors—continue to travel with these and other organizations to diverse areas of the globe. They exemplify the institution's central values of compassion, dignity, integrity, and service. They offer medical education, technology, medicines, and a helping hand to people who cannot repay them. Through their efforts, the goal of changing and improving the lives of the less fortunate becomes ever more a reality.

Anyone wishing to share in Fairview's sponsorship of these volunteers can contact the Foundation and designate donations for medical missions.

Fairview Foundation
2450 Riverside Avenue
Minneapolis, Minnesota 55454
www.fairview.org/foundation
Tel. (612) 672-7777
Fax (612) 672-7776